Callimachus

ANCIENTS IN ACTION

Boudicca, Marguerite Johnson
Cassius Dio, Jesper Majbom Madsen
Catiline, Barbara Levick
Catullus, Amanda Hurley
Cleopatra, Susan Walker and Sally-Ann Ashton
Hadrian, James Morwood
Hannibal, Robert Garland
Homer, Jasper Griffin
Horace, Philip D. Hills
Lucretius, John Godwin
Marius, Federico Santangelo
Martial, Peter Howell
Ovid: Love Songs, Genevieve Lively
Ovid: Myth and Metamorphosis, Sarah Annes Brown
Pindar, Anne Pippin Burnett
Pliny the Elder, Aude Doody
Protagoras, Daniel Silvermintz
Sappho, Marguerite Johnson
Spartacus, Theresa Urbainszyk
Tacitus, Rhiannon Ash
Thucydides, P. J. Rhodes
Virgil, Jasper Griffin

Callimachus

Richard Rawles

BLOOMSBURY ACADEMIC
LONDON • NEW YORK • OXFORD • NEW DELHI • SYDNEY

BLOOMSBURY ACADEMIC
Bloomsbury Publishing Plc
50 Bedford Square, London, WC1B 3DP, UK
1385 Broadway, New York, NY 10018, USA

BLOOMSBURY, BLOOMSBURY ACADEMIC and the Diana logo are trademarks of Bloomsbury Publishing Plc

First published in Great Britain 2019

Copyright © Richard Rawles, 2019

Richard Rawles has asserted his right under the Copyright, Designs and Patents Act, 1988, to be identified as Author of this work.

For legal purposes the Preface on p. vi constitutes an extension of this copyright page.

Cover design: Terry Woodley
Cover image © Werner Forman / Getty Images

All rights reserved. No part of this publication may be reproduced or transmitted in any form or by any means, electronic or mechanical, including photocopying, recording, or any information storage or retrieval system, without prior permission in writing from the publishers.

Bloomsbury Publishing Plc does not have any control over, or responsibility for, any third-party websites referred to or in this book. All internet addresses given in this book were correct at the time of going to press. The author and publisher regret any inconvenience caused if addresses have changed or sites have ceased to exist, but can accept no responsibility for any such changes.

A catalogue record for this book is available from the British Library.

Library of Congress Cataloging-in-Publication Data

Names: Rawles, Richard (Richard John), author.
Title: Callimachus / Richard Rawles.
Description: London : Bloomsbury Academic, 2019. | Series: Ancients in action | Includes bibliographical references and index.
Identifiers: LCCN 2018048683 (print) | LCCN 2018052252 (ebook) | ISBN 9781474254878 (epub) | ISBN 9781474254885 (epdf) | ISBN 9781474254854 (pbk.) | ISBN 9781474254861 (hardback)
Subjects: LCSH: Callimachus—Criticism and interpretation. | Greek poetry–History and criticism.
Classification: LCC PA3945.Z5 (ebook) | LCC PA3945.Z5 R39 2019 (print) | DDC 881/.01—dc23
LC record available at https://lccn.loc.gov/2018048683

ISBN: HB: 978-1-4742-5486-1
       PB: 978-1-4742-5485-4
       ePDF: 978-1-4742-5488-5
       eBook: 978-1-4742-5487-8

Series: Ancients in Action

Typeset by RefineCatch Limited, Bungay, Suffolk
Printed and bound in Great Britain

To find out more about our authors and books visit www.bloomsbury.com and sign up for our newsletters.

Contents

Preface ... vi

	Introduction	1
1	Callimachus on Philology and Poetics	15
2	Callimachean Voices	45
3	Religion and the Gods	65
4	People and Places	91
	Envoi: The End of the *Aetia*, and Callimachus in Rome	115

Notes ... 127
Bibliography ... 133
Index ... 137

Preface

This book started life at the suggestion of Roger Rees, to whom I am very grateful. I would also like to thank Alan Griffiths, in particular for his class on Hellenistic Poetry at University College London, one of the most important I attended, and students at St. Andrews, Nottingham and Edinburgh with whom I have read Callimachus since then. For reading and supportive comment and much else besides I would like to thank Lucia Prauscello, Alison and Stephen Rawles, and Antonia Ruppel.

The reader for and editorial staff at Bloomsbury have been consistently helpful, and considerate in the face of delays and repeatedly missed deadlines.

Responsibility for error or folly remains my own.

Introduction

Callimachus, his life and his times

Callimachus described himself for posterity in two sepulchral epigrams. Probably neither of these was composed for inscription on an actual tomb; rather, he uses the form of inscribed epigram in order to explore a way of describing and defining an identity in a brief, pithy way. The first is presented as an epigram for his father (21 Pfeiffer = 29 Gow and Page):[1]

> Whoever you are walking past my tomb, know that
> I am both son and father of Callimachus of Cyrene.
> You should know of both: one once led his country
> in battle; the other sang songs more powerful than envy.

According to the common Greek practice, Callimachus was named after his grandfather: the latter had been a general of Cyrene, whereas the former was great as a singer, which is to say a poet. Callimachus stresses his own achievement in poetry and his grandfather's as a soldier serving Cyrene (while, in a sign of the artificiality of the form, nothing is said of the father himself, notionally the speaker of the epigram: presumably a 'real' epigram for the father's tomb would have been different). The second epigram is for Callimachus himself (35 Pfeiffer = 30 Gow and Page):

> You are walking past the tomb of Battiades, skilled at
> song, and at timely laughter mixed with wine.

Callimachus calls himself by the name 'Battiades' to claim descent from Battus, the semi-mythical founder of the Greek colony of Cyrene. Again, his own claim to fame is in poetry (again described as 'song', as it would be in a poet of an earlier period), as well as the gracefully appropriate wit associated with the traditional *symposion* (ritualized drinking party). When Callimachus sums himself up in this form, then, he emphasizes his own ability as a poet, presented in a traditional mode as a 'singer' (the word is the same used for bards in Homer), as one with the manners of a gentleman, and in particular as a man descended from the most noble family of Cyrene.

As we shall see, Callimachus' working life is particularly associated with Alexandria; his birthplace, Cyrene, although also in North Africa, had a rather different history. Cyrene was a Greek colony founded many centuries before (the traditional date is 631 BC), by Battus (also known as Aristoteles), who led a colonizing party from the small island of Thera in the southern Aegean. It therefore had a much longer history than Alexandria, which had been founded by Alexander the Great (in 331 BC, i.e. in living memory for much of Callimachus' life). Cyrene also had a distinguished mythical and poetic heritage, particularly in the form of songs by Pindar for Cyrenean athletic victors (*Pythians* 4, 5 and 9), all three of which treat the mythical history of the colony (particularly associated with Apollo, also a significant presence in Callimachus' poems).

However, while Cyrene was Callimachus' birthplace and his Cyrenean heritage was important in his self-presentation, he seems to have spent much of his life in the new city of Alexandria. Alexandria was itself new – but it also belonged to a new world. In the archaic and classical periods, the political and military history of Greece was dominated by the *polis*, the city state. In Callimachus' lifetime and afterwards, it was dominated by a small number of powerful monarchies controlling huge swathes of territory with the use of mercenary troops. Why was it so different? In a word: Alexander. During the fourth century, Macedonia, a previously rather marginal area to the north of peninsular Greece, became increasingly powerful under its king, Philip II, and defeated a coalition of Greek states at the battle of Chaeronea (338 BC) to become in effect master of mainland

Greece. After the death of Philip in 336 BC, his son Alexander ('Alexander the Great') took power, and embarked eastwards and southwards on an extensive campaign of military conquest, becoming master of what had been the Persian Empire, including Egypt. His eastward expedition took him as far as India; he died in Babylon in 323 BC.

After Alexander's death, the huge empire he had conquered fell to pieces, and after some confusion the western end of it became dominated by a number of monarchies carved out by his generals and associates from the empire Alexander had left behind. From the 270s BC throughout Callimachus' life, the most important of these were the Seleucids (descendants of Alexander's general Seleucus), controlling a vast territory (it got smaller over time) from Asia Minor through to India; the Ptolemies (descendants of Ptolemy I 'Soter', 'the Saviour', another associate of Alexander who managed to obtain his body after his death), based in Egypt with Alexandria as capital, but with fluctuating control over other areas in the eastern Mediterranean and Asia Minor; the Antigonids (descendants of Antigonus Gonatas), based in Macedonia and with considerable power over mainland Greece; and among smaller kingdoms most important for our purposes is a later dynasty of the Attalids (descendants of Attalus, a noble Macedonian by ancestry, who inherited the kingship of Pergamum in 241 BC).

Callimachus' career, as both poet and scholar, was closely associated with the Ptolemaic capital in Alexandria. He did scholarly work at the library there, and a number of his poems praise and commemorate Ptolemaic kings and (particularly) queens. It is not completely clear how to reconcile this with evidence of recurrent conflict between the Ptolemies and his native Cyrene in the period from 275 to 246 BC, when Magas ruled Cyrene independently despite having been sent there by Ptolemy I to govern on his behalf. It seems hard to imagine that he spent all of this period in Cyrene and none of it in Alexandria, but (unsurprisingly, perhaps, since most poems by Callimachus are impossible or difficult to date) we have few poems clearly dating from this period that explicitly show Ptolemaic allegiance (probably only the *Apotheosis of Arsinoë*, fr. 228 Pfeiffer, which must have followed fairly soon after her death in 270: other datable poems either pre-date or post-date Magas' secession). His active career seems to have lasted from the 280s to the late 240s BC; he was probably born towards the end of the fourth century. Independently of his works, other information about his life is very hard to come by (and many traditions about his life are probably false): an interesting detail which may be true is reported by the twelfth century AD scholar John Tzetzes (we do not know his source), that Callimachus was a royal page at the Ptolemaic court (i.e. the court of Ptolemy I). Several poems by Callimachus are strongly marked by a relationship with the court, such as the *Apotheosis of Arsinoë* (fr. 228 Pfeiffer), which commemorates the death of Arsinoë II, both wife and sister of Ptolemy II 'Philadelphus'; the *Victory of Berenice* at the beginning of the third book of the *Aetia*, commemorating the victory of Berenice II, wife of Ptolemy III, in the Nemean Games; and the *Lock of Berenice* at the end of *Aetia* 4, commemorating a military triumph of her husband.

Why was Ptolemy II married to his sister? This requires a further discussion of the culture of Ptolemaic Alexandria. After the death of Alexander, the Ptolemies made their capital in this new city in a very old territory, and the majority of the population of Egypt was Egyptian rather than Greek in language and culture. However, the Macedonian Ptolemies (as Alexander had before them) wanted to assert their cultural Greekness in the Hellenic world at the same time as governing a non-Greek people. They sought to control Egypt through attracting a Greek governing class, at the same time promoting their monarchical status to both Greeks and Egyptians. Thus the king was 'Pharaoh' to the Egyptians, and among the more surprising customs of Pharaonic monarchy that the Ptolemies adopted was the practice of royal brother–sister incest (the marriage of Ptolemy II 'Philadelphus' to his sister Arsinoë seems to have provoked at least a frisson of controversy among Greeks, who reached for the brother–sister marriage of Zeus and Hera as a mythological parallel: see below, pp. 24–5, on *Aetia* fr. 75.4–9 Pfeiffer). The institutions and habits of Egyptian religion were maintained. At the same time, however, the kings presented themselves to the wider Greek world and to the Greek settlers whom they sought to attract to Egypt as Greek kings, of Greek heritage and culture.

To this end, the Ptolemies acted as patrons of cultural activity on a colossal scale, and spent lavishly to make Alexandria a cultural hub in the new 'Hellenistic' world ('Hellenistic' is the modern term for the world after Alexander, in which large swathes of territory were 'Hellenized', i.e. developed Greek cultural characteristics as a result of his conquests). This may have been inspired by the cultural patronage of Macedonian kings (Philip II of Macedon brought Aristotle to his court to serve as tutor to the young Alexander), which itself belonged to a longer tradition of Greek monarchy, as seen for example in the patronage of poets by Polycrates of Samos and the sons of Peisistratus in Athens in the sixth century BC, and by Sicilian tyrants' patronage of poetry (including drama) in the fifth century, but it was also highly innovative in scale and institutional form. Many places in the Greek world were the site of a *Mouseion* ('Museum'), i.e. a shrine for the worship of the Muses. In Alexandria, a *Mouseion* was founded by Ptolemy I as a new kind of institution, though still formally organized as a religious shrine: a kind of research college for scholars and scientists, appointed and funded by the king. Here scholarship included mathematics and natural sciences of many kinds (including medicine) as well as the study of literature. Ptolemy I probably also founded the famous library (if not he, then his son): again, there are precedents in the history of Greek monarchy for book collections (and Ptolemy may have been inspired by libraries in the Near East), but in the Greek world the Alexandrian library was innovative both in institutionalization and in scale. There was a serious attempt to compile a complete library of Greek culture insofar as it could be represented in books.

An anecdote survives according to which Ptolemy III 'Euergetes' persuaded the Athenians to lend him their official performance texts of the three great classical tragedians, Aeschylus, Sophocles and Euripides, giving the enormous sum of fifteen talents as security; when the books arrived, he had them copied and returned the copies, telling the Athenians to keep the fifteen talents (Galen, *Commentary on the Epidemics of Hippocrates* 2.4). This story tells us something of the collecting fervour with which the Ptolemies sought to build up their collections, rather as the wealthiest museums have done in modern times; it also may show something of a new attitude towards texts, by which scholars wished to have access to the 'best' sources. Scholarship on texts included 'textual scholarship' in the narrower sense: scholars were confronting the problem that manuscripts contain errors and differ from one another, so that an editor must make judgements about the 'correct' text to be transmitted (as well as dealing with other problems like false attributions of works to authors, etc.). It may be for this reason that the Athenian copies of the tragedians were particularly sought after; in any case, scholars in Alexandria (including Callimachus) were concerned with establishing correct texts of classic authors and with working out how to classify the wealth of literary works which had been inherited from all over the Greek world.

Callimachus himself was part of this world. Although most scholars believe that accounts according to which he was himself librarian are based on misunderstanding, he certainly worked extensively in and on the library. In particular, he was the author of the *Pinakes* ('lists'; more literally, 'tables'). This work was described in the *Suda* (a Byzantine encyclopaedia, drawing on otherwise lost ancient sources) as 'Tables of those who were distinguished in every kind of literature and of what they wrote, in 120 books'. This work seems to have performed the functions of a library catalogue combined with those of a systematic bibliography of pre-existing literature, divided into genres (such as 'rhetorical works', 'epic', 'history', etc.). Within genres alphabetical order seems to have been used. Callimachus was faced with problems such as determining the genre of a poem found in a manuscript (is this a paean? ... a dithyramb?), as well as confronting questions of the type 'is this really by Sophocles?' He cannot have confronted every problem of this kind in the minutest possible detail (otherwise it could never have been done in one lifetime, even in 120 books), but this must still have entailed an enormous amount of work and an amazing degree of immersion in the whole of Greek literature as it had been transmitted. It is likely that Callimachus' work lies in the background of many of our later sources for Greek literature. Even if none of his poetry had survived, he would deserve an honourable place in the history of Greek scholarship and the transmission of knowledge about Greek literature.

We also have (again mostly from the *Suda*) some titles of scholarly works by Callimachus, of different kinds. 'Local names' presumably dealt with differences in vocabulary between the Greek *poleis*, and seems to have been organized thematically (we have a fragment about the names of species of fish: 406 Pfeiffer); other titles such as 'concerning winds' and 'concerning birds' may refer to sections of it. We know of a work 'Foundations of islands and cities and their changes of name'. This is not a complete list: but it is striking that these works seem already to show a possible overlap with areas of interest in Callimachus' poetry, and more generally an interest in obscure vocabulary that is also visible in the poems.

Above I have emphasized changes between the archaic and classical periods on one hand, and the Hellenistic period on the other; I have emphasized innovation and difference and even rupture between the world before Alexander and the world after. Awareness of this kind of change, however, must be tempered with awareness of historical continuity. If we think only in terms of contrasts between the world of Hellenistic poetry (bookish, scholarly, based on writing rather than performance) and the world of earlier poetry (oral, embedded in public social institutions, performative, civic), we are likely to end up with a misleading caricature of both. The archaic and classical periods were not a straightforwardly 'organic' folk culture; rather, poets engaged with each other's work and with traditions in self-conscious and sophisticated ways that imply an awareness of and reflection about canons, traditions, innovations and so on; complex metapoetics and patterns of allusion can be found in Pindar, in the dramatists, perhaps especially in Aristophanes; poets composed for occasions and with a view to performative communication, but also for posterity with a view to reperformance in unpredictable circumstances, and no doubt in many cases with a view to a transmission in writing and as part of a canon of successful works. Euripides (especially as received in the comedies of Aristophanes) can seem like a rather 'Hellenistic' figure, bookish and intellectual, for all that his plays were composed for public performance to a mass audience, and we will see that Callimachus' presentation of his own poetics implicitly identifies Aristophanes' Euripides as a predecessor (see below, pp. 32–3).

Just as aspects of poetics that might be seen as characteristically 'Hellenistic' are already visible in the archaic and classical periods, so the institutions of earlier times particularly associated with poetry continued to exist in the time of Callimachus. Festivals with poetic competitions (including the dramatic festivals of Athens); the *symposion* (ritual drinking party); choruses worshipping the gods in song and dance: all of these things were still a part of the world of Hellenistic Greece (indeed, in many cases our evidence for them is actually rather better in later than earlier periods, thanks to the survival of inscriptions). As so often, we need to try to temper awareness of change with awareness of continuity. The world of Callimachus is not the same as the world of archaic and classical times, and Hellenistic poetry shows differences from the poetry of earlier periods. However, these differences, in society and in poetry, are sometimes differences of emphasis and degree. They may also represent differences in our responses, conditioned by scholarship that has tended to read Hellenistic poetry for intertextuality and metapoetics, while more freely relating earlier poetry to performance and society, and to religion, history and other such 'big questions' – of course, these are questions which can and should be asked of Hellenistic poetry too, including Callimachus.

Callimachus' poetry

This book is mostly concerned with Callimachus' poetry rather than his scholarship. Sadly, much of his most important work is available only in fragmentary form; but over the past century the quantity available has become much greater thanks to the publication of papyri. Here, I briefly outline and describe his output.

Works preserved complete

Six *Hymns* by Callimachus have survived in their entirety. They did so by 'piggy-backing' in the same medieval manuscripts as the so-called Homeric Hymns, i.e. hexameter hymns from the archaic period, which were an important generic model. Apart from the fifth hymn (to Athena), all are in the same dactylic hexameter metre, as used in the Homeric Hymns and in epic poetry; the fifth hymn, perhaps more innovatively, is in elegiac couplets. It is probable that the order of the six hymns was designed by Callimachus.

The other complete poems we have are epigrams: short poems, usually in elegiac couplets, in a tradition that reaches back to a mixture of short sympotic elegies and inscribed poetry (epitaphs and other kinds of inscription). These have mostly survived in the *Palatine Anthology*, an enormous collection of epigrams by poets from the archaic period through to the middle ages, itself compiled from several earlier anthologies. Callimachus' epigrams from this source are complete poems; on the other hand, if we had a copy of Callimachus' own book of epigrams we might well count the arrangement of such a book as part of the artistry of composition (and the interest of reading), so in a sense the transmission of these poems through anthologies is in its way still a process of fragmentation of the original Callimachean design.[2] We also have some fragments of epigrams which did not make it through this process of excerpting.

Fragments

With the exceptions indicated above, Callimachus' works were not transmitted through medieval manuscripts in the same way as, for example, the *Iliad* and *Odyssey* or the seven surviving plays of Sophocles. They have survived only in fragments, preserved in one of two ways. Either another text (which *has* been preserved through the middle ages) quotes or tells us about a poem by Callimachus, or a papyrus has been discovered and published which preserves Callimachus' words. I say 'a papyrus' as a kind of shorthand: in fact one of the best ancient witnesses to Callimachus is a wooden tablet on one side of which an ancient scribe wrote part of Callimachus' *Hecale* (see below, pp. 41–3, on this 'Vienna tablet', carrying fr. 260 Pfeiffer = frr. 69–70 and 73–4 Hollis). In some cases, scholars have managed to identify overlaps between multiple sources and a fragment may be made up from several sources; for example, in Hollis' edition of the *Hecale*, the fragments of columns from the Vienna tablet overlap with several quotations from the *Suda*, with a number from scholia (marginal notes in a manuscript derived from ancient commentary) on the *Iliad* and on other ancient works, two from the grammarian Herodian, and three different papyrus fragments in a complex and fascinating jigsaw by which the other sources add considerably more to the text visible on the tablet alone. The amount we know about these works varies enormously from case to case (and has changed a lot as a result of papyrus finds). The list below follows the arrangement of the standard edition of the Greek text by Rudolf Pfeiffer (the numbers of fragments in this edition, from 1949, are still the ones most commonly used in scholarship, and are the ones I have used in this book except in some places where the discovery of new evidence since his edition makes this impossible).

Aetia. This word is the (Latinized) plural of the Greek word *aition*, whose sense overlaps with English 'cause, origin, explanation' (cf. English 'aetiology'). This work, in four books, was a collection of elegies (a form defined by its couplet metre), each of which describes the origin or cause of something (usually a local custom of some kind). For example, the first *aition* in the first book was concerned with the question 'why do the Parians sacrifice without *auloi* [double-oboe: the main wind instrument in the Greek world] or garlands?', and the answer was a mythical story about Minos of Crete and the death of his son Androgeos. The first two books were organized as a dialogue between the narrator and the Muses, where he asks them various questions of this sort which they answer, while the third and fourth books lacked this kind of 'frame', instead consisting of a sequence of elegies on aetiological themes. Since datable references identified in books 3 and 4 are later than those in books 1 and 2, it may be that the explanation for this difference is that Callimachus first composed the first two books and then added books 3 and 4 later in life, dispensing with the frame of his original design; some who believe this also argue that it might have been at this point that he added a 'prologue' to the new four-book composition, at the beginning of book 1. This was Callimachus' magnum opus and his most famous work in antiquity. The state of preservation varies a lot from part to part, and the survival of a *diegesis* ('summary'/'synopsis') on papyrus helps us to reconstruct the sequence of stories.

Iambi. A collection of poems in iambic metres. The first announces itself 'Listen to Hipponax!' and thus marks this archaic iambic poet as a model; however, the subjects of the poems seem to be much more various than what we can see in the (meagre) fragments of Hipponax. The state of preservation is patchy (we know them mostly from papyri).

Hecale. This was Callimachus' epic – but a mini-epic, in one book. It was also the composition most concerned with Athens and Attica. It treated traditional heroic and mythical subject matter, an episode from the life of Theseus; but the main emphasis was not on Theseus' defeat of the bull of Marathon but on the old lady of the title in whose house he stayed on his way to find it. We have many short fragments from *Hecale* but few long ones; the most extensive are the astonishing and wonderful fragments from the 'Vienna tablet' mentioned above.

Miscellaneous. We have fragments of (and ancient testimony about) various other works, most in epic or elegiac metres (in the case of elegies it is possible that some of these once fitted into the *Aetia*).

Further reading

On the Hellenistic world, Alexandria, and the world of Callimachus

The first part of Gutzwiller 2007 is useful, as are essays in Clauss and Cuypers 2014 and the first part of Bing 2008; analysis of sources on Callimachus' life in Cameron 1995, which is also useful for its revisionist account of Hellenistic literary culture more broadly, and in the introduction to Acosta-Hughes and Stephens 2012. On Callimachus, Alexandria and the library Pfeiffer 1968 is still very useful; see also relevant sections of Reynolds and Wilson 1991; at much greater length, Blum 1991.

Acosta-Hughes, Lehnus and Stephens 2011 is a large and useful edited companion.

Callimachus' works (editions and translations)

The standard edition (in Greek only, with Latin notes) is Pfeiffer 1949–53, and the numbers of fragments in this edition are used in this book as in most other secondary literature.

Epigrams are sometimes cited by the numbering in Pfeiffer, but sometimes from Gow and Page 1965 (which includes commentary, but is not very accessible without knowledge of Greek). I use both numbers. Gow and Page is the numbering used in Nisetich's translation (below).

Stephens 2015 is an extremely useful edition of the *Hymns*, with introduction, translations and commentary. Harder 2012 is a huge and magnificent book: a text of the *Aetia* with introduction, translation and extensive commentary. It is mainly intended for readers with Greek, but the translation and intelligently structured commentary make it useful (selectively) for those without. The *Iambi* are given with facing translation and full discussion in Acosta-Hughes 2002. The *Hecale* edition Hollis 2009 includes an appendix of translations; the commentary is excellent but heavy going without Greek.

Nisetich 2001 is a very useful and carefully presented translation of (most of) the complete works and fragments, with running explanations of fragmentary texts as well as notes 'at the back of the book'. Lombardo and Rayor 1988 is attractive to read but only includes a small selection of the fragments. The *Hymns* and epigrams are included in the Loeb volume Mair and Mair 1955 and fragments in Trypanis, Gelzer and Whitman 1975.

1

Callimachus on Philology and Poetics

We have seen in the introduction that Callimachus' world was, among other things, a world of scholarship, and that Callimachus himself was a scholar of literature and part of the world of philology. How, if at all, is this engagement with the world of the library at Alexandria visible in his work as a poet? And how does he engage with the literary and aesthetic debates and disputes that have often been asserted as a conspicuous feature of the world of Hellenistic scholarship and poetry?

Epigrams on writing

We start with a relatively straightforward example. When Callimachus was compiling the *Pinakes* (his extensive catalogue and guide to the literature in the library), he will have had to make judgements about editorial problems such as 'who is really the author of this poem?' (or 'is this poem really by so-and-so?'). This kind of problem is turned into poetry in the following epigram, where the speaker is a book (*Epigram* 6 Pfeiffer = 55 Gow and Page):

> I am the work of the Samian who once received in his house
> the godlike bard; I commemorate Eurytus and his sufferings,
> and fair-haired Ioleia, and I am called a Homeric
> book – for Creophylus, dear Zeus, a big deal!

We are to imagine this written on a copy of the *Sack of Oichalia* by Creophylus; the work is identified as part of the world of reading and writing ('a Homeric *book*').¹ An early reader would probably encounter it in a book of epigrams by Callimachus (or read out from such a book), so must work out during the course of the little poem what is going on, and in the Greek as in my translation the key name 'Creophylus' is left until the last line. Creophylus was an epic poet of Samos (in some traditions Chios) and one of the Homeridae, a guild of bards associated with the early transmission of epic poetry, including Homer. He was believed to have been an associate of Homer himself, his friend or even son-in-law; Callimachus says that he entertained Homer in his house. The *Sack of Oichalia* told of Heracles' sack of the city of which Eurytus was king, and the abduction of Eurytus' daughter Ioleia. So for a learned reader the details given in the first two and a half lines are enough to identify the work. Only at the end does the point become clear: some attributed the *Sack of Oichalia* to Homer himself. In other circumstances one might expect a poet to be annoyed that his work is attributed to another – but Creophylus is so much a lesser figure than Homer that in this case it is an honour! Our poet is a discriminating figure and knows better than to accept the false attribution. Here, presented with a light touch, is the sort of information which might be involved in an entry in the *Pinakes*: some biographical tradition about the author, the subject matter of his work, and the correction of a misattribution. But in the epigram it is transformed into a miniature puzzle and a sly joke about the hierarchy between the ordinary and the great: what a coup for Creophylus, that people took his work for Homer's – even if this might have erased altogether his own name, which Callimachus can restore to him!

In another epigram, we see Callimachus as thoughtful critic, praising a contemporary poet, Aratus of Soloi (*Epigram* 27 Pfeiffer = 56 Gow and Page):

> The song is Hesiod's, and so is its manner, but not Hesiod
> all the way; rather, I venture, the man from Soloi
> has taken an impression from the most honey-sweet of his verses.
>   Hail,
> delicate discourses, symbol of Aratus' sleeplessness!

Aratus, the author of a learned didactic poem about astronomy and meteorology, modelled on Hesiod, is praised, and praised in a way which demonstrates Callimachus' understanding of his poetic technique with the insight of a practitioner and critic. He has imitated Hesiod, but selectively; the subtlety of his work illustrates the work involved (sleeplessness represents late nights stargazing – and also polishing his poem). This is a poetics of polish, and of intelligently selective imitation of the poetry of the past.

Callimachus could censure as well as praise. This fragment (398 Pfeiffer) comes from an otherwise lost epigram:

> the *Lyde*, a fat piece of writing, and unclear

Here Callimachus criticizes Antimachus' *Lyde*, a work we know only from fragments, consisting of a catalogue of unhappy mythological love affairs to console the poet for the loss of his girlfriend, Lyde.[2] Antimachus worked in the late fifth/early fourth century BC, and was popular among the first generation of Hellenistic poets (he was praised by Asclepiades and Posidippus in epigrams: *AP* 9.63 = Asclepiades 32 Gow and Page; *AP* 12.168 = Posidippus 9 Gow and Page = Posidippus 140 in Austin and Bastianini 2002).[3] Callimachus, however, rejects his work as 'fat' (this is a literal translation of the adjective παχύς (*pachus*); like English 'thick' it can also mean 'stupid', and it sometimes seems to imply 'florid, excessive' or 'rough') and 'unclear'. This fits into a contrast between size, fatness, bloatedness, and subtlety and intelligence expressed on a smaller scale, which is a recurring theme in Callimachus' poetics. Also characteristically, the *Lyde* is described as *writing* rather than song (γράμμα, *gramma*).

Apollo in his *Hymn*

The next text we will consider has become a famous example, and may again involve a response to Antimachus. In the *Hymn to Apollo*, Callimachus starts by setting the scene: we are at a festival, and waiting for an epiphany of the god (1–8). How will he manifest himself? Another question is raised at lines 30–1, where the narrator is anticipating a choral performance in honour of the god:

> Nor will the chorus sing of Phoebus for one day only,
> for he is rich in song: who would not sing easily of Phoebus?

The assertion that Apollo provides so much material for song that a chorus will sing for more than a day about him makes one wonder about Callimachus' hymn: given the huge quantity of possible material, how will his poem ever end? The answer comes more than seventy lines later, after praise of Apollo for his various roles, a narrative concerning the establishment of the festival of Apollo Carneius in Cyrene, and an account of the origins of the ritual cry *hie, hie, paieon*! At this point, fairly suddenly, the poem ends like this (105–13):

> Envy spoke secretly in Apollo's ear:
> 'I do not admire the singer who sings not as much as the sea.'
> Apollo kicked Envy and spoke as follows:
> 'The stream of the Assyrian river is big, but it drags along
> many scourings from the land and much rubbish on its water.
> To Deo the Melissae do not bring water from everywhere,
> but the little stream that comes up pure and undefiled
> from a holy spring, the choicest essence.'
> Farewell, Lord! As for Blame, let him go where Envy dwells!

Both questions are answered together: despite the possibility of a song long enough to take more than a day, Apollo suddenly appears as the voice to mandate the curtailment of the much shorter poem, and two problems are neatly solved. Envy (Φθόνος, *Phthonos*) is a regular adversarial force in celebratory and praise poetry already in Pindar, whose songs frequently compete with the grumbling of envious people (φθονεροί, *phthoneroi*). The poetics of size is explored through water. Envy conveys the idea poetry should be big' by saying it should be 'as much as the sea' (in one influential but controversial reading 'the sea' is held to signify Homer, and we are concerned with the right way to respond to Homeric epic).[4] Apollo, kicking him, clearly rejects this, but reframes the idea as a contrast between two forms of fresh water. The Assyrian river is the Euphrates: though big, it is polluted and dirty. By contrast, the Melissae ('Bees': a name for priestesses of Demeter) bring water to Deo (Demeter) from a source which is small, but pure and a perfect example of its kind. A similar metapoetic contrast seems already to be attested, again in Pindar (at the very end of the second Partheneion, fr. 94b.76–7, where the context is fragmentary, but the chorus is told to avoid salt water).[5]

Much of this metapoetic passage, then, has good precedent, and also seems specifically motivated by the needs of this song: it provides the anticipated epiphany and explains and motivates the end of the hymn. For all that, it can *also* be read as a more general statement of poetics and an intervention in a broader aesthetic dispute: Callimachus takes the opportunity to strike a blow in favour of an aesthetic of smallness and perfection rather than imperfect, polluted bigness. This sense of a more general aesthetic intervention, perhaps rather different from what we find in Pindar or elsewhere in the archaic and classical tradition, may be visible in a feature that has recently been observed in lines 108–10.[6] Here a line which begins with A (for Ἀσσυρίου, *Assyriou*, 'Assyrian') is followed by two lines beginning LY and DE (λύματα, *lumata*, 'scourings' and Δηοῖ, *Dēoi*, 'to Deo'). This might operate as a subtle acrostic pointing to Antimachus' *Lydē* (perhaps associating it with the dirty river Euphrates). This is remarkable – but acrostics are not unknown in poetry of this period (the most famous is at Aratus *Phaenomena* 783–7),[7] and represent another way in which Hellenistic poetics engages more with the world of books and written texts: acrostics must be *seen* rather than heard. It suggests a much more esoteric engagement in poetics (but, importantly, a reader who 'misses' the acrostic can still make sense of the text). It also suggests that the passage should be read as a more general intervention in the poetic debate of these times, one in which responses to Antimachus are a particular bone of contention: it does not seem that the *Lyde* is *specifically* relevant to the context in this hymn, except because it has to do with the distinction Callimachus is interested in between short, refined work and longer, less 'pure' writing.

Loving books

The elegy *Acontius and Cydippe* was part of the third book of Callimachus' *Aetia*, and was a love story. Here we see engagement with scholarship and the world of the library embedded in a larger context. We have more surviving lines of this elegy than any other from the *Aetia*, and can fill in the gaps in the plot from later sources. Acontius, a young man from Ioulis on the island of Keos, saw and fell in love with Cydippe, of Naxos, when he saw her at the festival of Apollo on Delos. Love inspired him with a clever trick: he wrote on to an apple 'I swear to Artemis that I will marry Acontius' and rolled the fruit in front of Cydippe's servant, who picked it up and (being illiterate) asked Cydippe to read the inscription aloud, which she did. Having returned home, Cydippe was to be married, but repeatedly fell ill before her wedding; meanwhile, Acontius was suffering from his love for her. Cydippe's father asked the oracle at Delphi why his daughter kept falling ill, and Apollo replied that she was bound by her oath to Artemis and instructed her father to marry her to Acontius. He did so, and (we might say) they 'lived happily ever after', as well as representing the origin of the Acontiad clan at Ioulis: this seems to be the main *aition* ('origin, explanation': as explained in the introduction, the *Aetia* is a collection of such 'origins') in the story.

The plot feels like a charming, 'pretty' love story, and also relies on literacy, reading and writing. The beginning of the elegy survives, addressed (line 5) to Apollo (fr. 67.1–14):

> Eros himself taught Acontius, who burned with love for beautiful
> Cydippe – a boy in love with a maiden –
> a trick (for *he* was not cunning!), so that he might be called
> throughout his life the name of 'husband'.
> He, Cynthian lord, came from Ioulis, and she came from Naxos,   5
> to your sacrifice of oxen on Delos,
> one a descendant of the clan of Euxantius, the other of Promethus,
> fair stars of the islands both!
> When Cydippe was still little, many mothers for their sons
> asked for her as a bride in exchange for horned oxen;   10
> compared with her, no other girl went to hairy old
> Silenus' watery spring
> with a face so much like the dawn,
> nor placed her foot in sleeping Ariadne's dance.

As well as an interest in curious traditions (what is the watery spring of hairy old Silenus, and the dance of sleeping Ariadne?), we see the tale being set up as an almost clichéd 'boy meets girl story' (line 2); the emphasis on the noble ancestry of these 'fair stars of the islands' has something of the flavour of the 'handsome prince and beautiful princess' of later European fairy-tales.

The end of the elegy is startling (fr. 75.44–77; the beginning of line 59 is illegible on the papyrus):

In my judgement, Acontius, in exchange for that night
when you touched her maiden's girdle,   45
you would not have accepted the ankle of Iphicles, who ran on the
    corn-ears,
nor the wealth of Midas of Celaenae,
and they will bear witness to my judgement
whoever is not ignorant of the harsh god.
From that marriage a great name would come about,   50
for still your clan, the Acontiadae,
inhabits Ioulis, rich in number and honours,
Cean, and we heard of this your desire
from ancient Xenomedes, who, once upon a time,
set down the whole island in a mythological memoir,   55
beginning with how it was inhabited by Corycian nymphs
chased from Mount Parnassus by a great lion,
(for this reason they call it Hydroussa), and how Cyrene's
[...] lived in Caryae,
and how people settled there from whom Zeus   60
Alalaxios receives sacrifices accompanied by the cry of trumpets,
Carians together with Leleges, and how it was given its changed name
by Phoebus' and Melia's son Ceos.
He put insolence and death by lightning, he put the sorcerer
Telchines, and he put in his tablets the old man Demonax who,   65
in his madness, cared nothing for the blessed gods,
and he put the old woman Macelo, mother of Dexithea:
only these two, when the gods destroyed the island for wicked
insolence, did they leave unscathed.
And he told how, of the four cities, Megacles built   70
Carthaea, and Eupylus, son of semi-divine Chryso,
built the citadel of Ioulis with its many springs, while Acaeus
built Poeessa, shrine of the Graces with beautiful hair,
and Aphrastus the town of Coresius, and he spoke, Cean,
of your bitter love mixed with the story of these,   75
that old man devoted to truth, from which the boy's
story ran to our Calliope.

As elsewhere in the elegy there is a contrast between different kinds of knowingness and expertise. The narrator implies that, as Acontius, he too has experience of Eros (line 49: only those who are ignorant of love would disagree), and this combines with the direct address (line 44) to Acontius in a way that suggests a kind of sympathy and understanding between narrator and character. This sympathy based on shared erotic experience is immediately followed by an astonishing moment as the narrator explains the source of his own story, in a book: the elegy ends with a long footnote! Callimachus not only explains that the story comes from Xenomedes' history of the island of Ceos, a work of the fifth century BC now lost to us, but he also gives us a potted summary of the content of the work, in which the story of Acontius was 'mixed' with the stories of the island's four cities – from which Callimachus himself has un-mixed it! We see that the work of Xenomedes offered a wide choice of *aetia* ('origins, explanations') among its variety of local mythology and foundation stories ('why do the Carians and Leleges sacrifice to Zeus Alalaxios with the accompaniment of trumpets?', 'how did the island of Ceos get its name?', etc.). In part, then, Callimachus is demonstrating to us how his own work in the *Aetia* is the result of a process of selection from the much broader category of possible *aetia*.[8] This is a striking example of the foregrounding of research – of scholarly activity as part of the process of poetic composition. The contrast with earlier and alternative models of poetic inspiration (and with the first two books of the *Aetia*, in which the narrator portrayed himself in dialogue with the Muses) is especially marked at the end, where we see that the story of Acontius, rather than being transmitted from Muse(s) to poet, has instead 'run' from the book (the work of Xenomedes) to the Muse Calliope.

The startling final 'footnote' fits into a pattern of ways in which the narrator is characterized by his learning and knowledge and in which this characterization is juxtaposed and contrasted with the story that he tells. The narrator knows a great deal from books, but as we have seen he also wants to present himself as in sympathy with the erotic feeling of Acontius by appealing to the common understanding of all who have experienced love. Callimachus the poet, Xenomedes his source and Acontius his subject matter are all writers (Xenomedes is shown as such with the mention of writing-tablets at fr. 75.66 [65 of my translation]; Acontius writes on the apple, and is also shown writing Cydippe's name on the bark of a tree in fr. 73). The narrator's insistence on the youth of Acontius and Cydippe suggests that we perceive him as considerably older; Xenomedes is 'ancient' (fr. 75.54: it combines the idea that he lived in the past and that he was an old man). This contrast in ages overlaps with a contrast between the erotic world of Acontius and the world of curiosity and learning associated with the narrator, despite his eagerness to identify with Acontius' erotic desire.

The narrator is characterized both as knowledgeable and as enthusiastic and eager in the pursuit and display of knowledge: this enthusiasm can be compared with the erotic zeal of Acontius. We can see this at the beginning of the same long fragment containing the end of the elegy. These lines describe how Cydippe became ill on the day she should have married, but begin with a curious feature of wedding ritual on Naxos, which the narrator is about to explain before he stops himself (fr. 75.1–15):

> ... and already the maiden had slept with a youth,
> since there was a custom ordering the bride to spend the night
>   before the wedding
> with a male child, both of whose parents were living.
> For, they say, once Hera – dog, dog, hold back, shameless
> spirit! You will sing even what religion forbids!   5
> It is fortunate that you have seen nothing of the rites of
>   the dread goddess,
> or you would have spewed out their story too.

> Indeed much knowledge is a terrible evil, if somebody cannot
> hold his tongue. Truly, this child has a blade!
> The oxen of the morning were ready to tear their hearts   10
> upon glimpsing the sharp knife in the water.
> But in the afternoon a terrible pallor took her and sickness came,
> that sickness which we send away to the wild goats
> and call it 'sacred': but this is a lie! This grievous disease
> wasted the girl away almost to the house of Hades.   15

First we see another possible *aetion*: why was it the custom on Naxos for a bride to spend the night before her wedding with a boy both of whose parents yet lived? Our knowledgeable narrator has an answer, which (we are to understand) would have involved reference to the incestuous pre-marital sex life of Hera and Zeus, her brother and later husband: but this is too shocking and he startlingly interrupts and chastises himself (in lines 6–7 he says that it is just as well he has not been initiated into the secret mysteries of Demeter, otherwise he might have disclosed that information too). The same indiscriminate enthusiasm for display of his own knowledge is part of the narrator's characterization again where he describes Cydippe's disease: something similar to what we call 'epilepsy' was commonly referred to in Greek as 'the sacred disease' and treated by a form of exorcism by which the malady was cast out of the patient's body on to goats (compare the miracle of Jesus where demons are cast out on to pigs: Matthew 8: 28–34; Mark 5: 1–20; Luke 8: 26–39). One of the medical treatises of the corpus attributed to Hippocrates concerned this disease ([Hippocrates] *On the Sacred Disease*), and countered the traditional wisdom by arguing that the disease was not at all 'sacred' but should, on the contrary, be explained 'scientifically'. The learned narrator is so keen to show his knowledge of this that he has forgotten the meaning of Cydippe's sickness within the story! In this case it *is* a 'sacred disease', and its function is to delay her wedding until her oath to Artemis can be fulfilled.

The narrator's delight in obscure lore and learning is replicated in his delight in unusual vocabulary (this is harder to see in translation). For example, in line 9, he uses a proverb, whose usual form is 'Don't give a knife to a child!' (it is used where somebody has more of something than he can handle). But normally the regular word μάχαιρα (*makhaira*) is used for 'knife'; here the proverb is spiced up with the much rarer μαῦλις (*maulis*); two lines below, at 11, the same ordinary word for a knife is avoided (in the description of the oxen who see a reflection of the sacrificial knife in the bowl of water used during the ritual), this time in favour of δορίς (*doris*), again a rare synonym for 'knife', found for the first time in attested Greek here.

In addition to these interactions with prose literature and delight in obscure vocabulary, Callimachus is also interacting with the verse tradition – but doing so in a way which seems to reflect a new, 'scholarly' style of reading. In the third line of the elegy (fr. 67.3, quoted above) we are told of Acontius 'for he, at least, was not πολύκροτος (*polykrotos*)': above I translated 'for *he* was not cunning'). The word is difficult to translate: since it is found as an alternative reading to πολύτροπος (*polytropos*) in the first line of the *Odyssey*, which means 'cunning', one might expect *polykrotos* to mean about the same. On the other hand, in other places it seems to mean something like 'talkative'. Perhaps (as suggested in the commentary by Harder on this line) we should understand that both senses are present here: Acontius lacks cunning *and* fluency in speech, both useful traits in a lover.[9] But the way in which the 'he' of this phrase is emphasized suggests something more here (my use of italics for '*he*' represents the Greek particle γε, *ge*: more literally, 'he, *at least*, was not *polykrotos*'). 'Acontius, *at any rate*, was not *polykrotos*' suggests 'even if somebody else may have been'. That somebody, surely, is Odysseus: as I have mentioned, *polykrotos* is recorded as an alternative reading in place of *polytropos* in the very first line of the *Odyssey*, describing that poem's hero. We cannot be sure that this reading is older than Callimachus, but it is plausible that it should be so, and this passage arguably attests to it. As we have seen in the introduction, Callimachus was a scholar as well as a poet. He and his contemporaries were among the first systematically to address the problems of the variable transmission of manuscript texts, which frequently present this kind of problem: should this word in the first line of the *Odyssey* read *polytropos* or *polykrotos*? For the first time scholars were engaged in the same activity that is a characteristic preoccupation of classicists now: the production of scholarly editions, requiring choice between textual variants. With this single ambiguous word, then, Callimachus plays on knowledge by some readers of textual difficulty in the first line of the Homeric *Odyssey*: whether or not Odysseus was *polykrotos*, Acontius was not. Thus the narrator displays his knowledge of and delight in the details of textual scholarship, and Acontius' relatively minor and less heroic story is compared with that of Odysseus: Odysseus was cunning, and he certainly had 'the gift of the gab', and he was also successfully a husband, which is the goal of Acontius. The reader is presented with puzzles: what is the right word in the *Odyssey*, and what does it mean here? Acontius' world and his story, where the written text of a few words on an apple is so important, is contrasted with the world of a different kind of writing: scholarship and books in the library.

This elegy, set up from the start as a cute love story, is also a key example of the importance of learning and scholarship in Hellenistic poetry, and in Callimachus in particular, perhaps most spectacularly so for the expanded 'footnote' at the end. With this as our example, we can see that such interaction between poetry and scholarship is neither dry nor tedious. On the contrary, the interplay of overlaps and contrasts between the world of the enthusiastically learned and knowledgeable Callimachean narrator and the world of his characters is a key source of the humour and poetic interest of the elegy. The narrator's love of learning and interest in the lore of the past, from mythology to medicine to ritual to the details of Homeric textual criticism, is a part of the play of characterization in the poem rather than simply reproducing the preoccupations of a scholarly author. As the characters – and Acontius in particular – act out their passionate story of a cunning erotic plot, so the narrator acts out his passionate enthusiasm for knowledge of books, of words, of stories: the poetry happens as these two worlds meet.

Beginning the *Aetia*

The passage usually known as the '*Aetia* Prologue' (fr. 1 Pfeiffer) combines the two concerns of this chapter: it is an important example of how we can see Callimachus sorting through and thinking with exemplars of poetry from the past, in a way which it is easy to connect with the importance of scholarship in Alexandrian intellectual culture and in his own life, and it shows how he expresses a view of poetics of the same sort as we saw in the final lines of the *Hymn to Apollo*. This passage stood at the beginning of the first book of the *Aetia* (the *Aetia* seems to have been composed in two stages, with the first two books early in Callimachus' career, and books 3 and 4 added later; it may be that it was at this later stage of composition that the prologue was added, though the self-presentation of Callimachus as an old man might well be a poetic fiction).

This amazing passage is rich in both difficulty and interest. Our text comes from papyrus, and some parts are missing: [square brackets] surround words which are entirely or largely supplemented to fill gaps in the text; unfilled gaps are indicated like this: [...].

> Often the Telchines murmur against me and my singing
> – fools, who are no friends of the Muse! –
> because I did not accomplish a single, continuous song, either
>   [the deeds]

of kings, in many thousands of lines,
or the heroes [of the past], but I [roll out] my speech on a
    small scale 5
like a child, though my count of decades is not small.
[Well, I say] this to the Telchines: '[Thorny] tribe,
knowing [only] how to waste away your own livers'
[I may well be] of few lines. But the nourishing Lawgiver
greatly outweighs the long [...]; 10
of the two, the tender [...] teach that Mimnermus is sweet,
but the large woman does not.
[A long way,] from Egypt to the Thracians, let the crane fly,
delighting in the blood of the pygmies,
and let the Massagetae shoot arrows a long way against 15
[the Mede; nightingales] are sweeter like this.
Go away, you destructive race of malice! From now on,
judge poetry by skill, not by the parasang!
Do not seek for a loud, clattering song born of me:
it is not for me to thunder, but for Zeus!' 20
When for the very first time I put a writing-tablet on my lap
Lycian Apollo said to me:
'[Remember, dear] singer: raise your sacrifice as fat as possible,
but, good fellow, keep your Muse slim.
This also I enjoin upon you: to tread where wagons do not go, 25
nor to drive your chariot on the common tracks of others
nor along the wide road, but on untrodden
paths, even if you drive on a narrower one.'
I obeyed. For we sing among those who love the clear sound
of cicadas, and not the din of donkeys. 30
Like the long-eared beast let another bray –
I would be the small, the winged one!
Ah, totally – old age! dew! – may I sing
while eating dew as free fodder from the clear sky;
may I shed old age, which now is a weight upon me 35
like the triangle island on destructive Enceladus!
[...] for when the Muses look not askance on one as a child,

they will not reject him as a friend when he is grey.
[And when Apollo's swan can] no longer move its wing,
[... its voice] is then clearest. 40

The elegy is presented as a reply to critics, described as 'Telchines': mythological prehistoric metal-workers, probably dwarvish, associated with magic, malice and envy (compare fr. 75.65 where we find Telchines on Ceos; they are also associated with Rhodes). Already in antiquity people tried to identify these with historical contemporaries of Callimachus, but it is unclear whether the Telchines should be identified with specific people. In any case their role here is to allow Callimachus to explore the poetics of the *Aetia* in a programmatic fashion at the start of the collection. The way in which the critics are called Telchines and described (line 2) as 'fools, who are no friends of the Muse!' gives a passionate and aggressive tone from the start, and this sense of strong emotional engagement by the narrator continues, but co-exists with a subtle and ambiguous presentation of his own poetics.

The contrast initially presented is between 'one single, continuous song' on heroic or royal subject matter (lines 4–5), which the Telchines wanted, and the smaller scale production they consider child-like, despite the narrator's advanced age (lines 5–6). It is tempting to perceive a contrast between Callimachus' elegiac *Aetia* and epic poetry in the Homeric tradition, not least because rejection of epic is important in passages of Roman poetry which allude to this prologue (see below, pp. 121–4); yet Callimachus' reply points in a different direction.

Lines 9–12 are difficult, and controversial: the gaps in the papyrus cover key nouns (and perhaps even complete this would have been hard to understand!). What I suggest here is one of a number of possible interpretations.[10] In lines 9–10, the narrator says that a work known as the 'Lawgiver' (*Thesmophoros*: a title of Demeter) is better than another (its name is missing), described as 'long'. In the next couplet (lines 11–12), there is again a contrast: of two works or collections, one ('the tender [...]': the missing noun is plural) teaches us that Mimnermus is sweet, but another, known as 'the big woman', does not. A fragment of ancient commentary preserved on another papyrus helps: 'he makes a comparison of the poems of few lines by Mimnermus of Colophon and Philitas of Cos, saying that they are better than their poems of many lines' (Florentine *scholia* 12–15).[11] The 'Lawgiver' refers to the *Demeter* (a poem we know about from other sources) of Philitas, an older contemporary of Callimachus: an elegiac poem. In my view, the easiest interpretation which coheres with the sense of the ancient commentary (if it is correct) is that Philitas' *Demeter* is compared with some other, longer, work by the same poet. In the next couplet, following the same logic, it seems that a work by Mimnermus (another elegiac poet, but much earlier, from the seventh century BC) known as 'the big woman' does not illustrate that poet's 'sweetness'; 'the tender poems' (or something of the sort), on the other hand, do. In my view, the 'big woman' probably represents Mimnermus' *Smyrneis*, a long elegy treating the mythical and historical story of the city of Smyrna (Mimnermus' work was collected in two books, the *Smyrneis* and another named *Nanno* after his female beloved: the latter is probably the collection called 'tender' poems by Callimachus).

Despite the angry start of Callimachus' poem, which might lead us to expect a simple binary ('I am right; you are wrong'!) we now see a more subtle and complex set of critical judgements, based on a full knowledge of elegiac tradition: the superiority of shorter elegies is shown *within* the works of both Mimnermus, a poet of many centuries earlier, and Philitas, a figure of living memory. Both poets composed short and long elegies, but in the view of our discriminating narrator both are better in their shorter works. The contrast between elegy and epic does not seem relevant, since, if we are concerned with genre at all, we seem to be dealing with different kinds of elegy, but we may be more concerned with stylistic differences that can operate across genres: we shall see that both dramatic and lyric voices are also present. The narrator's angry polemic is supported by subtle argument based on discriminating judgement about poetry of the recent and distant past.

In the lines that follow, we have a sequence of things which may and should be 'long': the migration of cranes, and the arrow-shots of the Massagetae, a people to the North of the Caspian (cf. Herodotus 1.201–14 for their conflict with the Medes, i.e. Persians). These serve as foil for 'nightingales', i.e. poems, which should be shorter (the same metaphor is found at *Epigram* 2.5 Pfeiffer = 34.5 Gow and Page). The imagery coheres in two ways: the large (cranes) compared with small (nightingales) birds, and the cranes who famously fought battles with the pygmies of Africa juxtaposed with the similarly warlike Massagetae (for the cranes, compare *Iliad* 3.2–7: Callimachus describes the South to North migration of Spring, and Homer the North to South migration of Autumn). As we go on, length is combined with noise. The part of the elegy addressed to the Telchines ends with an injunction to judge poetry by 'skill' rather than by the 'Persian σχοῖνος (*schoinos*)', a long eastern unit of measurement (translated as 'parasang' above), before the sphere of comparison changes from size to sound: 'Do not seek for a loud, clattering sound born of me: it is not for me to thunder, but for Zeus!' The kind of poetry rejected is both over-long and noisy: this comparison is prepared for with a possible contrast of noisy cranes with sweet-voiced nightingales (Homer's cranes are noisy: Callimachus' implied reader knows this).

At this point (line 21) there is a change of course, but continuity of imagery eases the transition. The narrator recalls a poetic initiation in the form of an epiphany of Apollo (he, rather than Zeus, is the god of poetry) that took place early in his life ('When for the very first time I put a writing-tablet on my lap': note again the interest in *writing*). Apollo repeats the idea of preferring smaller to larger poetry by saying that the poet should make his sacrifices fat, but his Muse slim. We may remember the 'large woman' ('fat woman'?) of Mimnermus, rejected in line 12, and also an earlier text that focused on issues of poetics. The latter part of Aristophanes' *Frogs* is taken up with a contest between Aeschylus and Euripides in the underworld. Here Euripides describes how he changed the Aeschylean type of tragedy which he had inherited by making it lose weight (Aristophanes *Frogs* 939–43: the word translated as 'art' is feminine in gender, which makes the metaphor of a woman's body easier):

EURIPIDES: At the very point when I first received the art from you
she was swollen with bombast and fattened with wordiness.
I immediately reduced the swelling and slimmed her down . . .

In the contest of the *Frogs*, between the grand and bombastic Aeschylus and the subtle and intellectual Euripides, Callimachus seems to align his own poetics with Euripides as he maps his disagreement with the 'Telchines' on to the contrasted poetics presented in Aristophanes' play.

As we continue, the range of imagery broadens: as well as the contrasts between long and short, noisy and sweet-sounding, we have the image, common in Greek as in English, of a contrast between paths or roads (in Greek, e.g. Hesiod *Works and Days* 287–92; Robert Frost's 'The Road Not Taken' was published before the first edition of the papyrus from which we know Callimachus' elegy). Callimachus' poetry should be exclusive and far from the crowd, and should embrace novelty ('untrodden paths') even if this is somehow restrictive. Even where the imagery describes and advocates novelty, however, it is also traditional and evokes past treatments of poetics: not only is the underlying scheme of 'contrasted paths' deeply traditional, but the idea of a song or poem as a chariot and of rejecting the well-trodden road is already present in a passage from a song of Pindar (*Paean* 7b, 10–12):

> Sing out hymns
> not going on the well-trodden wagon-road of Homer
> but with another's horses

The details of Pindar's lines are uncertain and the context fragmentary, but we can see that even where Callimachus announces his own novelty he is still looking to the poetry of the past and to past treatments of the question how to relate to the poetry of the past. In addition to the elegies of Mimnermus and Philitas, and comic responses to tragedy, Callimachus' elegy evokes also Pindar's lyric response to Homeric tradition.

The following eight lines (29–36) are one of the most astonishing passages in Greek literature. The cicada, an insect like a tree-living grasshopper, makes a 'crick crick' noise by vibrating a membrane in the thorax. This sound was perceived by the Greeks as 'song': another 'singing animal' like the nightingales of line 16. It was believed to live by eating dew, and to be capable of rejuvenation by shedding its skin.

The comparison with the unmusical donkey is traditional, found in a fable attributed to Aesop: the fable of the ass and the cicada (184 Perry) tells how the donkey asked the cicadas what they ate, that they could sing so well; upon hearing their answer the donkey tried to emulate them by living only on dew, and starved.[12] Unsurprisingly, then, Callimachus' narrator prefers the cicada, and implicitly casts his rival poets (noisy, big) as donkeys. But the analogy, by which 'good' poetry is like the sound of the cicada, and 'bad' poetry like the braying of donkeys, is transformed: suddenly the narrator wishes actually to *be* 'the small, the winged one', and the analogy is turned into a wish for metamorphosis, by which the narrator himself can eat dew and shed old age as the cicada does. We were told at the beginning (line 6) that 'my count of decades is not small', and now we find that his desire for rejuvenation is because old age is weighing him down like 'the triangle island' on Enceladus (Enceladus was a giant buried under Mount Etna on the 'triangle island' of Sicily).

The idea of metamorphosis into a cicada opens up a new range of mythical and poetic resonances. It suggests the myth of Tithonus, a beautiful young man who was abducted to Olympus by the goddess Eos, the dawn. When she had taken him there, she persuaded Zeus to grant immortality to him – but forgot to ask for perpetual youth! As a consequence, Tithonus grew always older but without dying, and Eos loses interest in him as he loses all of his faculties except for his voice. What happens next varies between versions, but Callimachus has in mind a story by which he is metamorphosed into a cicada, which (thanks to its ability to shed its skin) is repeatedly rejuvenated instead of growing old, and has its voice for ever as a producer of everlasting song.

The combination of the idea of the ageing poet with the Tithonus story is strongly suggestive of Sappho's poem treating the same ideas, of which (since 2004) we now have almost the entire text:[13]

> [Be eager,] young ones, for the fair gifts of the violet-breasted Muses,
> and the clear-voiced lyre which loves singing.
> [As for me,] old age has now seized my skin, once [tender],
> and my hair, once black, is white.
> My spirit is made heavy, my knees do not carry me,
> which were once nimble for dancing like fawns.
> These things I frequently mourn: but what can I do?
> It is not possible for a human to become ageless.
> They used to say that once rose-armed Dawn,
> [...] by love, went to the ends of the earth carrying away Tithonus.
> He was young and beautiful, but all the same grey old age
> grasped hold of him, who had an immortal wife.

It may be that Sappho already expects knowledge of the metamorphosis of Tithonus; if so, we might say that Callimachus makes explicit what Sappho leaves in the background. An alternative story of metamorphosis of people into cicadas, again with a clear musico-poetic significance, is told by Plato's Socrates at *Phaedrus* 259b–d: when the Muses came into being, some men were so addicted to song that they did not stop even to eat, and from them came the cicadas, who need no food but dew and sing constantly. Callimachus' lines evoke a mixture of traditions concerning metamorphosis, rejuvenation in old age, and song. Another passage of Plato has been suggested as a special presence in line 32, 'I would be the small, the winged one!' At *Ion* 534b, Socrates, in the course of arguing that the poet's knowledge is derived from inspiration rather than skill (the same word τέχνη, *techne*, as is used at line 18 of Callimachus' poem), says, '... the poet is a light, winged, holy thing, and cannot compose until he is inspired and frenzied and his mind is no longer in him'. The appeal to judge poetry by skill earlier in the elegy might seem to point to a conception of poetry as a matter of craft and technique rather than inspiration, but here the Platonic echoes point in another direction.[14]

Already in this line the asyndeton ('lack of connection': the absence of a word such as 'and') in 'the small, the winged one!' conveys an excited mood. In the lines which follow, as the idea of metamorphosis takes hold of the narrator, the syntax of the Greek goes wild (lines 33–6: it is not easy to translate in a way which reflects this!):

> Ah, totally – old age! dew! – may I sing
> while eating dew as free fodder from the clear sky;
> may I shed old age, which now is a weight upon me   35
> like the triangle island on destructive Enceladus!

After an initial exclamation (the opening 'Ah!' raises the emotional temperature), the narrator first names two grammatical objects in the order 'old age, dew' (the reader must think about how to relate these to what precedes, and to activate traditional knowledge about cicadas). Then there follows the clause 'may I sing ...', going with 'dew', and 'may I shed', going with old age (in my translation the nouns are repeated, where in the Greek they are not). The effect is disorienting and dislocated; it feels as if the narrator were overcome with emotion at the wishes he expresses, and the disjointed syntax suggests an extemporized and immediate form of expression, a poetry of inspiration and powerful emotional engagement rather than of carefully premeditated construction.

At this point (lines 37–40) the text starts to give out, but it looks as if we are getting to the end of the elegy or of a section within it, since the idea of friendship with the Muses in old age as well as childhood seems to pick up on ideas from the very beginning ('ring-composition'). The poet refers to the idea that the swan sings most beautifully at the end of its life as an analogy for his continued friendship with the Muses in old age. In the next elegy his relationship with the Muses was again stressed, as he narrated how as a young man he met the Muses of Helicon in a dream; his dialogue with them constituted the first two books of the *Aetia*.

Callimachus, we see, favours shorter, more delicate poetry over noisy and over-long writing. But he tells us this in a way which mixes an exuberant range of imagery and engages with a wide variety of earlier literature, both prose (Plato, Aesopic fable) and verse (comedy and tragedy, Pindar, elegists ancient and modern). The poet is expressing his own poetics by sorting through and discriminating between a range of poetry and poetics of the past: within the elegiac canon, Mimnermus and Philitas, centuries apart, both illustrate the superiority of shorter elegies to long elegiac narratives; the desire for metamorphosis into a cicada activates a range of texts including Sappho and Plato; Apollo's instruction to value novelty is expressed in a way that recalls Pindar's response to Homeric epic, and allusion and imagery combine to give the paradoxical sense that Callimachean novelty is itself expressed in a deeply traditional way. The poet can make selective and discriminating judgements about the literature of the past like a critic, and can draw on a wide range of literature in a way which suggests the books of a library, with multiple genres of verse and prose mixed together. Again Callimachus the philologist seems to shine through his poetry.

The instruction of Apollo again points to the word of books and writing: Callimachus is addressed when he starts to *write* (line 21: 'When for the very first time I put a writing-tablet on my lap'). Yet even though Callimachus identifies himself explicitly as a poet of the written word, this poetry still has much to do with the world of sound. Apollo speaks to Callimachus as he takes up his writing-tablet, but he addresses him with the word ἀοιδός (*aoidos*), 'singer', the same word used of bards in the Homeric poems (line 23). The poetry favoured by Callimachus contrasts with the poetry the Telchines want in aural qualities as well as length: they want loud, clattering song. The aural contrast between the 'clear sound' of the cicadas and the braying of donkeys is stressed by onomatopoeic writing, which I have tried to reproduce in the translation: 'Like the long-eared beast let another bray!' (line 31) renders a line which ends with a marked and emphatic rhythm of four consecutive long syllables on the verb ὀγκήσαιτο (*ongkēsaito*), suggesting the nasal honking or braying of a donkey, and in the same sentence the poet will *sing* among those who love the sound of cicadas. This poet of writing still has a lot to do with the world of aurality and orality.

The poetics of Callimachus here seem at first sight to align him with 'skill', (τέχνη, *techne*), as he tells the Telchines to judge poetry by 'skill' rather than length (line 18). Yet as the elegy continues we see that this call for a criticism focusing on 'skill' is not unambiguously matched by the way Callimachus presents himself as narrator and poet. In the astonishing lines on which I spent so much time above, the desire for metamorphosis into a cicada, we saw that his description of 'the small, the winged one' seems to recall Plato's account of the poet as a 'light, winged, holy thing'. Yet where Plato's Socrates says this, his whole point is to deny that a poet is possessed of 'skill': he means 'inspired *rather than* skilled'. It is at this point that the syntax of the Greek becomes so strange, as the narrator's powerful emotional engagement with the wish for rejuvenation and metamorphosis overcomes him, and the tumbling language suggests a 'Dionysian' poetics of inspiration rather than of the careful exercise of skill. Even the idea of Tithonus' transformation into a cicada, which can produce its song for ever, may seem to come oddly close to the poetics of the 'single, continuous song' which the Telchines wanted but the narrator rejected.

How should we make sense of this brilliant but complex presentation, which seems to include, if not contradiction, some inconsistency? Without seeking to deny that the historical Callimachus is using this elegy to participate in the poetic disputes and discourses of his own time, we should not treat this as simply versified poetics or theory, but as poetry and indeed as a monologue, which is to say a drama. We should look for poetic 'sense' rather than the argument of a prosaic philosophical treatise. In a way which has some similarities to my reading of *Acontius and Cydippe*, we should pay attention to the narrator as a character: how is this 'Callimachus', the speaker of the poem, presented to us? He is a character who is deeply, aggressively committed to his views on poetics: his critics are not just mistaken, but foolish Telchines and no friends of the Muse. His commitment to the poetics he espouses, a poetics of the small, the skilful, the light, is shown to us in the exuberant fullness and variety of the imagery and breadth of reference, which also itself represents a display of his skill and knowledge. His skill is also the skill of the philologist of the library: a full and discriminating knowledge of the literature of the past, so that his own poetic commitments are worked out and presented to us through both overt references and implicit allusions to previous texts.

This engagement with the texts and poetics of the past, however, is also an engagement with texts and poetics that are not *of* or *from* the library: the drama of Aristophanes and its engagement with the drama of Aeschylus and Euripides; the choral song of Pindar; songs of Sappho; Plato's inspired poet who composes for performance. The myth of Tithonus, used here as a poetic myth, is likewise a myth about a world of orality and performance, where Tithonus changes into an everlasting singing voice. Callimachus' 'philology' – his poetic and literary expertise, involving the world of the library, of writing-tablets, of careful reading and discriminating judgement – involves serious engagement and emotional commitment to this world which is not of the library. 'Philology' is etymologically 'love of speech/discourse/words,' just as philosophy is 'love of wisdom,' and here that idea of underlying emotional engagement that accompanies and psychologically motivates expertise seems deeply relevant: as we see from the vehemence of the narrator's wish to *become* the cicada and slough off old age, his commitment to the cicada, to rejuvenation and to song is an emotional one as much as an intellectual one.[15] He is committed to a poetics of skill, but also shows how deeply he is drawn emotionally to a poetics not only of smallness and skill but also of inspiration and performance and unending song. His inspiration from Apollo came when he first took up his writing-tablet, but his passionate desire is to become a voice of everlasting and rejuvenated song.

Callimachus and the philologists

How does this relate to us and *our* world? Callimachus was looking back at the world of Pindar, Sappho, Xenomedes, and others, across a gap of time, and doing so from a milieu in which these texts were approached from books and as part of a world of professionalized scholarship – how much more so are we, and across a much larger gap of time! Part of how we respond to Callimachus, then, may be affected by a perceived analogy between Callimachus' activities and interests and the activities and interests of modern literary scholars and, more broadly, the scholarly 'frame' in which we approach Callimachus (a frame made up of libraries, prose criticism, translations with notes, daunting editions with extensive scholarly apparatus, etc.). We may find it unsurprising that the most important modern editor of Callimachus, Rudolf Pfeiffer, was also a historian of classical scholarship. It is easy to see a kind of continuity or at least repetition between the scholarly world of the library as a presence in Callimachus' poems and the scholarly activity by which we can read them, especially as the latter is considerable: to an unusual though not unparalleled degree (and this is only intermittently visible to readers in translation) simply reading Callimachus is only possible because of intense scholarly activity. This is particularly true of the fragmentary works, known from papyri and quotations in later ancient authors: getting sense from these may involve much painstaking work on the amount of space for a gap (three big letters? four small ones?), identification of overlaps between quotations and letters preserved on papyri, attempts to read barely visible ink ..

This connection may be perceived especially because of the emphasis on the book or writing-tablet and the materiality of the written word which we have noted above, since so much of the scholarship by which we can read Callimachus has been about painstaking work on papyri, i.e. fragments from ancient books. While the *Hymn to Apollo* has survived complete through medieval tradition, our knowledge of *Acontius and Cydippe* and of the prologue to the *Aetia* is mainly derived from partially preserved ancient books. To take a particularly striking example, in the case of our largest and most interesting fragments from Callimachus' mini-epic, the *Hecale*, we are concerned with an ancient writing-tablet of the sort which Callimachus mentions as his own medium for poetic composition (the 'Vienna tablet': fr. 260 Pfeiffer; frr. 69, 70, 73 and 74 Hollis). The *Hecale* was not transmitted to us through medieval manuscripts, but we have many quotations in other ancient and medieval sources, as well as papyri and this writing-tablet. In fact, because he quoted from it, we can tell that a copy (probably complete) of the *Hecale* lasted as late as the beginning of the thirteenth century, in the possession of Michael Choniates, Archbishop of Athens (it was perhaps destroyed when the city was sacked in 1205 in the Fourth Crusade – otherwise we might well have had a complete text).

The wooden board was written on in ink in the fourth or fifth century AD and preserves four consecutive columns from *Hecale*, but they are very hard to read. In 1968, Hugh Lloyd-Jones and John Rea had re-edited the tablet from a photograph (Rea later consulted the original) and presented their work to colleagues in a research seminar. They had seen that previous scholars had failed to read the first line of the first column correctly. At this point, Theseus has just captured the bull of Marathon. For the second half of this line Lloyd-Jones proposed a reading which translates as 'his club had smashed the other': up to this time, nobody had supposed that Theseus used a club in this way. What about the beginning of the line? The traces here are astonishingly faint. M. L. West, working from a description of the ink, went away from the seminar to think through interpretations which might yield a plausible word or words, and proposed οἰόκερως (*oiokerōs*), 'single-hornedly': a very rare word indeed, but it fitted the traces and seemed to make plausible sense.

Lloyd-Jones' reading took advantage of a passage in the writings of Michael Choniates where he says that Theseus 'smashed the other of his horns with his club' (the same verb is used, and the same word for club). Meanwhile, the same word οἰόκερως (*oiokerōs*, 'single-hornedly') is found only in one other place in Greek literature – and then, unknown to West, in another work by Michael Choniates! So we have one more line of Callimachus to read, through a combination of determination and skill, confirmed by the close parallels in the work of a medieval cleric who almost certainly cannot have got this information and vocabulary other than from the last copy of the *Hecale*.

This kind of delightful (and geeky!) detail of brilliant success in the basic philological reconstruction of fragmentary material can help us to imagine that the suggestion of A. S. Hollis, editor of the *Hecale*, that while editing a fragmentary text 'one may feel inclined to adapt the words of St. Augustine, "Let a complete text of the *Hecale* be found, but not quite yet"', was partly derived from delight in fragments and working on fragments as well as from a desire not to see his reconstructions proved wrong by new evidence.[16] In addition to delight in philological ingenuity, one may feel a connection with the emphasis on the materiality of written texts as presented by Callimachus, as well as with Callimachus' poetics of intensely wrought small-scale work and attention to detail. Needless to say, not all of Callimachus foregrounds poetics or scholarship to the same degree as the texts I have selected for discussion in this chapter (nor are poetics and scholarship the only features of these texts worth discussing or enjoying); on the other hand, for many readers these moments may seem important in the way in which we attribute a personality and character to the Callimachus that seems to come out of the text.[17] This sense sometimes contributes, I suspect, to the evaluative reception of Callimachus by modern readers. Many readers may warm to a poet who, they feel, shares their own intense interest in linguistic detail, in books, and in literature of the past; on the other hand, others (or, indeed, the same people!) may feel that Callimachus feels too scholarly, too bookish, and lacks the sense which we may have when reading as it might be Sappho, or Homer, or Sophocles: a sense of contact with a living oral culture that takes us away from the books of the library to the world of song and performance and drama. As I have tried to argue, however, this feeling of an intense emotional engagement with the world of song, of performance, of the voice – all of this is also intensely present in the work of Callimachus and in his self-presentation in his own work. The scholarly and argumentative Callimachean narrator also craves metamorphosis into the cicada: the constantly rejuvenated creature of song.

Further reading

On Callimachus and his world, see also the reading suggested in the introduction. Bing 2008 (1st ed. 1988) is an influential approach to 'bookishness' in Hellenistic poetics, while Cameron 1995 takes a revisionist approach, stressing continuity. On archaic and Hellenistic narrators, Morrison 2007. For the *Hymn to Apollo* compare the approach of Williams 1978 with the successful counter-argument at Cameron 1995, 403–9 (but both are hard without Greek); Stephens 2015, 72–99 is friendlier and very useful. For all *Aetia* fragments, Harder 2012 is now crucial (also as a source of bibliography). On *Acontius and Cydippe*: Fantuzzi and Hunter 2004, 60–7, with further bibliography indicated at p. 61 n. 68. Useful treatments of the *Aetia* prologue: Acosta-Hughes and Stephens 2002; Acosta-Hughes and Stephens 2012, 31–47; Fantuzzi and Hunter 2004, 66–76. The re-reading of the Vienna Tablet of the *Hecale*, Lloyd-Jones and Rea 1969; for Michael Choniates and the *Hecale*, Hollis 2009, 38–40.

2

Callimachean Voices

We have seen the startling way in which, both in the prologue to the *Aetia* and in the Hymn to Apollo, Callimachus introduces the voice of Apollo as part of the presentation of his own poetic preferences and affiliation. In both cases, argument becomes a kind of drama, an interchange of voices; in the hymn, the vocal/aural presence of Apollo represents the epiphany for which we have been waiting since the start of the poem. We have also seen how, by my reading, the poetry of Callimachus' *Acontius and Cydippe* 'works' by playing on the contrast between the bookish narrator and the subject matter of his story: in other words, the narrator is an important character and 'voice' in the poem. Finally, we have seen how Callimachus' poetry rather frequently draws attention to the materiality of writing and reading, by referring to writing-tablets and books. Yet the poetry is rich in sound and in voices.[1] In this chapter, I explore the ways in which Callimachus' poetry creates a wide variety of voices, of narrators and characters, and in which it constitutes a repeated and sustained celebration of the power of poetry to make the voice come out of the written page.

The written voice

The focus on books and writing in Callimachus may seem innovative and characteristic of the age of the library, and to some degree it is. However, interest in the relationship between writing and voice was not invented by Callimachus or his contemporaries: from the beginnings of the alphabetic age, writers of Greek were fascinated in the relationship between material writing and speech. We first see this in inscriptions. The following may be our earliest Greek verse inscription, incised on an otherwise rather ordinary cup from a grave on the island of Pithekoussai (modern Ischia) from the late eighth century (454 *CEG*):

> I am the cup of Nestor, good to drink from. Whoever drinks from this cup, immediately desire of fair-garlanded Aphrodite will seize him.

If the first verb is correctly restored, the cup itself speaks to us, and the person who reads the inscription lends his voice to the cup. There is a contrast between the magnificent cup of the Homeric Nestor (*Iliad* 11.632–7) and the more humble cup bearing the inscription, and also added wit in the way in which the speaker of the lines is likely to diagnose his own wine-induced horniness. This cup is suggestive for the ongoing tension between accounts of Hellenistic poetry stressing rupture from the past and accounts stressing continuity. This is a metrically messy text on a rather humble object from a small colony in the very earliest stages of Greek alphabetic writing, yet it displays several characteristically 'Hellenistic' gestures: the eroticization of 'serious' mythology; the contrast of the big and grand with the small and humble; more or less self-conscious written-ness is characteristic of inscriptions from the earliest times, but often feels characteristically 'Hellenistic' when it spreads to other genres of poetry.[2] The verb 'I am' is unfortunately not certainly read here (there is a lacuna, and the letters surviving are consistent with other restorations), but it is a plausible restoration because this feature of the cup, i.e. that it speaks in the first person, is very characteristic of inscribed objects in the archaic period. They regularly tell the reader 'So-and-so dedicated *me*', '*I am* the memorial of so-and-so', etc.

Some inscriptions show much more explicit interest in this phenomenon of an object with a 'voice'. This is a dedication from Halicarnassus, dated c. 475 (429 CEG):

> Skilfully wrought voice of stone, say who set up this offering,
>   bringing delight to the altar of Apollo.
> Kasbollios, son of Panamye – if you urge me to speak out –
>   dedicated this tithe to the god.

The inscription is a dialogue between an imagined passer-by and the voice of the stone on which the inscription is carved.

Perhaps few (perhaps none) of Callimachus' epigrams were composed for inscription on real objects, as these were.[3] They will in any case have been composed with the expectation that they would also circulate in books. Some of them, however, continue this tradition of playing with the *idea* of an object whose inscription allows the production of a voice. *Epigram* 5 Pfeiffer (14 Gow and Page) is a long epigram commemorating the dedication of a nautilus, a sea-shell, as a gift for Cypris of Zephyrion, the deified queen Arsinoë II, from Selenaië; here I translate only the beginning (for more, see below, pp. 99–101).

> I am a conch of old, but now you have me,
> Cypris of Zephyrion, as the first dedication of Selenaië,
> a nautilus who used to sail the seas ...

The poem begins almost bluntly by identifying the first person speaker: 'I am a conch'. Selenaië's dedication is commemorated by giving a voice to the sea-shell itself; as the poem continues, much of it is taken up with describing the creature's former life upon the ocean. The poet can give a voice even to this creature; yet its loquacity comes at the point when it enters the world of people and human communication (we have no reason to imagine it chatting away while it floated on the sea), and the poem ends with the shell inviting Cypris (that is, Arsinoë) to be well-disposed to Selenaië.

Epigram 34 Pfeiffer (22 Gow and Page) also starts off as a dedication, this time to the bluff Heracles, who has little time even for the shortest poems:

> To thee, lion-strangler, boar-slaying lord, I, an oaken club, was dedicated
> by – who? – Archinos – which? – of Crete – I accept.

Heracles has no time even to wait for a second line before interrupting to demand the crucial remaining information (i.e. the identity of the dedicator). So while we first read this as an inscription written on the wooden club, that inscribed 'voice' is then treated as a 'real' voice speaking in real time, that another voice can interrupt. It adds to the amusing characterization of the taciturn, impatient Heracles (each of his interventions in the Greek consists of only one word, so that his voice contrasts with the expansive style of the first line) that he demands the dedicator's name at precisely the point where the syntax tells us that the club was about to name him anyway. 'It may be doubted', say Gow and Page dryly in their commentary, 'whether this is a genuine dedication'.[4] Nor does Archinos of Crete seem to be identifiable. If the epigram commemorates a real dedication, whether or not it was actually inscribed on or by it, then Archinos might be pleased that the response of Heracles is, in the end, 'I'll take it!' But the main *poetic* point of the epigram seems to lie in its play with the fiction of the speaking object and its voice, and its characterization of the laconic Heracles.

Missing writings

In this example (*Epigram* 15 Pfeiffer = 40 Gow and Page), the speaker is the reader of an epigram which we must construct from his reaction to it:

> Timonoe? But who are you? By the gods, I wouldn't have known you
> if the name of your father Timotheus had not been
> on the stone, and Methymna, your city. Ah, truly I say
> that your husband, Euthymenes, will be suffering greatly for his loss.

We are to imagine (the third line makes this clear with 'on the stone': the word is στήλη, *stēlē*, a flat surface for inscription) that the words are spoken by a reader of an inscription which says something like 'Here lies *or* here I lie, Timonoe, daughter of Timotheus, of Methymna, wife of Euthymenes' (if we imagine a verb it perhaps makes more sense in the first person: the reader is replying). Even though Timonoe is not a common name, he does not identify the woman from her name alone, but as he continues to read he realizes who she is by reading her father's name, the name of her *polis*, and the name of her husband. Perhaps part of the underlying point is to do with the visibility of memorials for women of elite status who are themselves not commonly visible when they are alive (we may think of the Thucydidean Pericles' statement that the greatest glory for a woman is to be the least spoken of among men: Thucydides 2.45); the man who sees the tombstone knows her male relatives rather than herself. Here the 'epigram' is a text that puts us in mind of the content of another, probably fictional, lost epigram.

In another text, an elegy from the third book of the *Aetia*, we find the same phenomenon at greater length (fr. 64: we have the beginning of the elegy, but the end is missing):[5]

> Not even Camarina would bring upon you such a disaster as the grave
> of a pious man moved from its place.
> For indeed my own tomb, built up in front of their city
> by the Acragantines, out of respect for Zeus god of strangers,
> was utterly destroyed by a wicked man – did you ever hear of   5

Phoenix, the bold leader of the citadel?
He built my tombstone into the rampart, and did not respect
the inscription saying that I, son of Leoprepes,
lay there, the holy man of Ceos, who first invented
the extra [letters], and the art of memory;   10
nor, Polydeuces, did he tremble at you and your brother, who once
brought me outside the house which was about to fall down
alone among the diners, when – alas! – the house in Crannon
collapsed upon the great sons of Scopas.
My lords . . .   15

This requires some glossing. There was a proverb, 'Do not move Camarina!' Its explanation was that the people of that city wanted to drain the lake beside it, also called Camarina. An oracle said 'Do not move Camarina!' but they ignored it, and the result was that the city was destroyed by enemies who could now more easily approach it over land. So the narrator says that to move the tomb of a righteous man is even more disastrous than that, and then continues by narrating the destruction of his own tomb outside the city of Acragas (modern Agrigento, on Sicily). A dead man is speaking through Callimachus' poem – but who? This becomes clear at lines 7–8, when the speaker describes his epitaph: the son of Leoprepes, said to have added extra letters to the alphabet, is the poet Simonides, active in the early fifth century BC. He was particularly associated with epigrams (many were attributed to him in antiquity), but no epigram *for* Simonides survives (though we have many epigrams for other archaic and classical poets).

In the latter part of the fragment, Simonides recounts what was a famous anecdote about his life (our best sources are Cicero, *de oratore* 2.86.351–3 and Quintilian 11.2.11–16, but as the presence of the story here shows it was much older than that): he was commissioned to compose a song for a Thessalian aristocrat, but when he presented the song the patron was dismayed that much of it was taken up with praise of the Dioscuri, Castor and Polydeuces, rather than with himself, and he paid Simonides only half of the agreed fee. Later, at a dinner, Simonides was called away from the table by a messenger telling him that two young men had come asking for him; he left the building and found nobody, but while he was outside the house fell down upon those inside, whose dead bodies were so mangled that they could not be identified. The Dioscuri had punished the Thessalians – and saved the poet. Simonides, being known as the inventor of memory systems, could remember the spatial arrangement of the diners, and this enabled their relatives to bury the bodies.

The elegy is rather like an epitaph: as some epitaphs do it preserves, through writing, the voice of the dead. It describes the speaking inscription ('the inscription saying that ...'). Yet it is not an epitaph, but rather the voice both describes the destruction of his epitaph and paraphrases its content. The story thematizes the importance of burial of the dead (with regard to both Simonides' tomb and the story of the house falling down) and the sacred role of the poet in relation to that: Simonides is a 'pious man' and the 'holy man of Ceos', and the Thessalian tale commemorates his close relationship with the Dioscuri so as to illustrate Phoenix's folly in failing to respect his tomb, given his closeness to the gods. It also explores the role of the poet in allowing the dead to speak again: a role normally associated with funerary epigram, where the tomb is accompanied by a perpetually reiterated voice generated by the reading of the inscription (this may be the voice of the dead person or of a passer-by or another). Yet in this case, while the epigram *does* survive in a sense (Simonides' paraphrase feels very close: perhaps he, as an expert in memory, *could* quote it exactly, despite the stone's destruction), its voice is not available to us, and Callimachus dramatizes its replacement with a Simonidean narratorial voice which is not produced from stone but from Callimachus' own activity as a poet, who can commemorate Simonides even in the absence of an inscribed memorial.

Epic voices

Fascination and delight in the capacity of poetry to make voices happen is a persistent feature of Callimachus' poetry, even where the epigrammatic tradition is not relevant. We can see this in his *Hecale*, a one-book epic poem available to us only in fragments. In this poem, the Athenian hero Theseus captures the bull of Marathon; but the largest part of the poem was not taken up with his heroic deed, but with his stay at the humble house of an old woman, Hecale, the night before (the epic 'model' for this is Odysseus' stay at the hut of the swineherd Eumaeus). When he returns from his adventure, Hecale has died, and Theseus establishes the festival of the Hecaleia in her honour. We have fragments (sadly rather small ones) from the conversation of Theseus and Hecale; it seems clear that Callimachus in this poem made full use of the tendency already visible in the *Iliad* and *Odyssey*, that epic employs direct speech extensively, in a way which serves to characterize the speakers. In these fragments, as interpreted and put in order by Hollis, the poor, elderly and solitary Hecale first explains that she was formerly wealthy, and then narrates how she met her husband.

41 Hollis (253.1–6 Pfeiffer)

My poverty is not ancestral; I am not a pauper
from my grandparents. If only, if only I had a third . . .

42 Hollis (253.7–12 Pfeiffer)

I was watching my threshing-floor as the oxen circled round it
when his horses carried him from Aphidnae, like [. . .]
[. . .] and the sons of Zeus [. . .]
I remember his beautiful [. . .] and
a mantle studded with golden clasps,
the work of spiders [. . .]

43 Hollis (293 Pfeiffer)

beneath it his tunic reached to the ground

44 Hollis (376 Pfeiffer)

whose hair was long with the blondest curls

45 Hollis (274 Pfeiffer)

and somehow for him too the soft down of his beard was new-spreading,
like the flower of helichryse

46 Hollis (304 Pfeiffer)

and around his head a new hat from Haemonia
went right around as a defence against
the noonday heat

If Hollis' reconstruction of the sequence is correct, there is probably little missing between these fragments. Even in their fragmentary state we get a sense of Hecale's 'voice'. We see her interest in wealth, not only in the insistence in 41 that she was not born poor and her proprietorial supervision of her own threshing floor (Hecale is an unusually active and powerful female; the description of her watching the threshers at work is perhaps reminiscent of the king watching the harvest on the shield of Achilles at *Iliad* 18.556–7), but also in the way she emphasizes the luxurious costume of the young man from Aphidnae, her future husband: she uses rare terms for his items of clothing (suggesting a connoisseur's interest) and stresses the fine quality of the golden fastenings; similarly, the detail that 'horses carried him' (i.e. he was on a chariot) is an indication of his wealth ('sons of Zeus' may also be an indication of status, meaning 'kings').

The connection between clothing, emotional recollection and marriage is already thematized in the *Odyssey* (especially the disguised Odysseus' description of his own clothes, and Penelope's reaction, at *Odyssey* 19.220–60). Hecale's 'spotlight memory' of this, the most important moment of her life, is accurate and detailed in a psychologically convincing way. In fr. 45 we see that the young and beautiful Theseus, to whom she is speaking, reminds her of her husband – 'for him too' must mean 'as for you now'– in a way which delicately suggests a degree of eroticism in her reaction to Theseus (one may think of the eroticism of the relationship between Odysseus and Nausicaa in *Odyssey* 6, but with genders and age difference reversed).

Hecale's emotional range is not confined to mourning and eros. Fr. 49 Hollis (~350, 294, 368 Pfeiffer, supplemented from a newer papyrus) probably describes the death of Hecale's younger son at the hands of Cercyon, who challenged his victims to wrestle him. Cercyon was slain by Theseus, but if this has already happened Hecale does not know it, since the last legible lines of the fragment are her fervent wish for his torture and death (lines 14–15):

> I myself would fix thorns in his shameless eyes
> while he lives and, if right allows, would eat him raw!

In similar circumstances, after the death of her son Hector, Hecuba said of Achilles 'I wish I could fasten on to his liver and eat it!' (*Iliad* 24.212–13), and Hecale's vehement desire for revenge seems to draw on the vengeful mothers of both the *Iliad* and the tragic tradition, while the desire to poke thorns into Cercyon's eyes seems more innovative (possibly there is a kind of redistribution of roles from the story of Odysseus and Polyphemus in *Odyssey* 9: Hecuba wishes to put out Cercyon's eyes, as Odysseus and his men put out Polyphemus' eye, but also to eat Cercyon alive, as Polyphemus ate Odysseus' men).[6] With 'if right allows' this is undercut with a note of unheroic anxiety in a strange and potentially amusing way; Hecale is both a furious tragic mother and an old woman anxious to do the right thing.

Hecale's voice and the characterization achieved by it was probably the most important and memorable aspect of the poem which took her name: the focus of epic is removed from men and from heroism, and placed on an elderly, poor woman. But the most surprising surviving parts of this poem feature another voice. The 'Vienna tablet', discussed above (pp. 41–3), preserves fragments of four columns of writing, with gaps between them, from the latter part of the poem. In the first of these, we find Theseus leading the defeated bull of Marathon, and the rejoicing of the people at his victory. After rather more than twenty missing lines, the situation has changed radically: we find a scene in which an elderly female crow is addressing another bird (we do not know what species). She first tells of how the daughters of Cecrops, contrary to the goddess's instructions, opened the basket in which Athena had concealed the baby Erichthonius; they did this while the goddess was absent from Athens, and the crow provoked Athena's anger by bringing her the unwelcome news. As the crow explains in the next column, this happened when she was a chick. The point must be to illustrate the idea that one should avoid being the bearer of bad news. Probably, therefore (this is Hollis' interpretation), the crow is advising her companion not to tell Theseus that Hecale has died (he discovers this in fr. 79 Hollis [262 Pfeiffer]). The crow expands on this in the following astonishing fragment, where the last column on the tablet overlaps with a papyrus as well as some quotations (74 Hollis [260.44–69, 346, 351 Pfeiffer, supplemented from a newer papyrus]):

> May I only have a defence against terrible hunger for my belly!
> ...
> But Hecale ... frugal [meal] ...
> ...
> porridge dripping barley-meal to the ground   5
> ... nobody will be present ...
> ... bearer of bad news. May you yet live

at that time, so that [you see]
  how the Thriae inspired this old crow!
  By my – no! my days are not yet gone! – by my wrinkled   10
  skin, by this here tree, dry though it be –
  not yet, breaking pole and axle,
  have all the suns set their foot in the west,
  but an evening will come, or night or day or dawn,
  when the raven, who now might compete with swans   15
  for colour, or with milk, or the foam of the wave's crest,
  will have gloomy plumage, black as pitch:
  this reward will Apollo give him for his message
  whenever he learns a nasty secret, about Coronis,
  daughter of Phlegyas, now with Ischys, breaker of horses.'   20

As she was speaking, sleep seized her; sleep seized the other as she listened.
Both slept: but not for long. For soon there came
the chill dawn, when the hands of thieves are no longer
abroad: already the lamps of morning shine,
and somewhere a man drawing water sings the well-song,   25
and the axle wakes a man with his house by the road,
shrieking beneath the wagon, and again and again
the smiths cause annoyance by asking for a light . . .

At the beginning of the fragment, the crow is probably remembering how she used to be able to eat from the crumbs of Hecale's humble food: Theseus was not the only beneficiary of her hospitality. At the end of her speech, however, the crow makes a prophecy to reinforce her argument (the Thriae were nymphs of Parnassus who practised divination): it is like a traditional use of myth, but with the temporal relationship reversed as the crow uses a prophecy rather than a story from the past to illustrate her point. From *our* point of view, the story is an *aetion*: how did the raven get its black plumage? The answer is that it was a punishment inflicted by Apollo when the raven brought bad news to him: that Coronis, while pregnant by the god, has slept with a mortal lover, Ischys. Before that, ravens had the purest white feathers!

The humble crow speaks with eloquence, passion and authority, swearing an extravagant oath by her own body and by the tree on which the two birds sit, and the idea 'time has not yet all passed' is expressed with ambitious elaboration. As often in *Hecale*, there is fairly overt interaction with Homer. In line 14 ('an evening will come, or night or day or dawn'), the crow reworks Achilles' prophecy of his own death (*Iliad* 21.111–13):

> a dawn will come, or an evening, or a mid-day,
> when somebody in the fighting will take my life too,
> either casting with the spear or with an arrow from the bow-string.

As if competing with the Iliadic line, the crow names four times of day to Achilles' three; in the crow's prophecy as in Achilles' the times of day are presented out of sequence. Achilles is refusing to spare Lykaon, a son of Priam: 'I too shall die, so why should you be spared?' is his argument. In the crow's prophecy the idea 'I too' also lies in the background: the point is that the raven, now white, will be black (as the crow is: white plumage is seen as desirable, and the crow envies the raven for it). Yet Achilles' speech is a stark, desperately serious recognition of mortality; by comparison, the crow's implied rivalry with the raven seems trivial.

Being an elderly, passionate female who talks into the night, the crow is a mirror of Hecale, but a distorted one. The world of the poem is expanded: the crow does not only echo human characters, but has her own world and her own concerns; we are invited to imagine her point of view, as that of a vividly presented 'character'. This is playfully elaborated at the end of the fragment, with the list of human-generated morning noises. People are accustomed to being woken by birds, but here we have a change of perspective: if the birds need to sleep in, as a result of staying up late as this pair has, they may be woken by human early risers.

Birds and bushes: voices in the *Iambi*

Callimachus' *Iambi* begin with the voice of a long-dead poet, Hipponax (a figure of the late sixth century BC) (*Iambus* 1.1–4):

> Listen to Hipponax! Really: here I am
> back from where they sell an ox for a penny,
> with iambics not singing a battle
> against Boupalus, but [...]

As in the elegy on the 'tomb of Simonides', Callimachus' poetic power can bring the voice of a long dead poet back to life (from Hades: food in the underworld was proverbially cheap). His Hipponax is a re-imagined, new Hipponax, whose voice exhibits both continuities and changes from the startling obscenity and anger of the archaic voice, and this too is shown from the start: he will not continue his anger against Boupalus, his enemy in his own poems, but will refocus his iambics in a new way. Unfortunately, we cannot see exactly what he says that he will do after he says that he will *not* sing against Boupalus (the papyrus gives out); when the text resumes he calls his audience to the temple of Serapis, where he narrates how Bathycles of Arcadia instructed his son to give a golden cup to the best of the seven sages.

Our best preserved *Iambus* is the fourth, which clearly exhibits Callimachus' interest in the power of poetry to make voices happen. We have a *diegesis* (a summary or synopsis on papyrus) for this poem, which tells us that at the start the poet (this suggests that the narrator could be identified as Callimachus, no longer representing Hipponax) was arguing with a rival when they were interrupted by a third person, Simos (this, 'snub-nose', looks like a nickname). The poet turned on him and insulted him, calling him 'Thracian' and 'boy-stealer', and then narrated a fable. The fable was the largest part of the poem, and most of it survives: it is an account of an argument between the laurel and the olive about which is the better of the two. The two trees differ from one another, and also from the birds of *Hecale*: they are most concerned with their own meaning and value in the sphere of people rather than with benefit to themselves. Thus the laurel points out that the prophet Branchos used laurel in curing the Ionians of the plague; that laurel branches are brought to Delphi from Tempe to be prizes for victors in the Pythian games; that the laurel knows nothing of pain and suffering, while the olive tree is associated with funerary ritual. The olive then makes her reply (*Iambus* 4.44–84):

> So much she said, and no more. And the mother of ointment
> replied to her, quite untroubled: 45
> 'Lovely lady, you have sung the loveliest
> of all my deeds last, like Apollo's swan.
> May I never tire of acting this way!
> When Ares destroys men, I
> accompany them and [...] 50
> below, [...] of the bravest, who [...].
> And whenever his sons bear white-haired Tethys
> to the grave, or old Tithonus,
> I myself go with them, and lie upon the road.
> From these I get more joy than you from your procession 55
> from Tempe. But since you mentioned
> this too, how, as a prize, am I not better
> than you? For the contest at Olympia is greater
> than that at Delphi. But silence is best!
> I shall mumble nothing good about you 60
> and nothing harsh. But look! Two birds
> have long been sitting in my branches
> and they're twittering away (what a pair of chatterboxes!):
> '... and who discovered the laurel?' 'Earth and [...],
> just like the ilex, the oak, the galingale, the pine.' 65
> 'And who discovered the olive?' 'Pallas, when she contended
> with the god of the seaweed over Attica,

and a man (but a snake below) passed judgement on these ancient
    ones.'
'One fall for the laurel! Of the immortals,
which one honours the olive, and which the laurel?'   70
'Apollo honours the laurel, and Pallas her discovery.'
'That's a draw: I make no distinction between gods!'
'What is the fruit of the laurel? What can I use it for?'
'Not for food, not for drink, not for ointment!
But the fruit of the olive: first the [...] mouthful   75
they call *stemphylos*, then the oil,
and then the *kolymbas* which once Theseus drank.'
'I'm calling that as a second fall for the laurel!
Now, whose leaves do suppliants hold up?'
'The olive's!' 'That's the laurel on the ground a third time!'   80
(Dear dear! They don't tire of chattering, do they?
Bold crow, how is your lip not sore?!)
'Whose stem do they preserve at Delos?'
'The olive's stem, which gave rest to Leto.
[...] citizens [...] the community   85
[...] the laurel garlanded him
[...] the olive, victorious in its shoot
[...] and upon the pear
[...] praise
[...] prophets   90
[...] nor upon the door-post
[...] I say, the laurel.'
She finished speaking, and the laurel's heart was pained
at what she heard, and more than before was aroused
a second time for battle, until [...]   95
a rough old bramble bush sprouting round a wall
spoke up (she was not far away from the trees):
'Wretched ladies, will we not stop and avoid delight
for our enemies, and not speak shameful,
unlucky words to one another, but [...]?'   100
The laurel looked at her with a scowl like a bull's

and said, 'You terrible disgrace!
Now *you* are one of us, are you? May Zeus
never allow *that*! You make me sick standing next to us!
[...] No, by Phoebus! No, by the Mistress   105
for whom the cymbals clash! No, by Pactolus!
[...]

In a humane spirit, the olive argues that her service to the dead and bereaved is a strength rather than a weakness (Tethys and Tithonus signify old age), and then picks up on the laurel's point, that she is the prize at Delphi, by noting that to be the prize at Olympia is even better (Olympic victors were garlanded with olive leaves). At this point, however, the olive stops arguing on her own behalf and claims to report the conversation she overheard between two birds. She presents this as an alternative to 'mumbling' praise or blame; it is a device to 'have her cake and eat it' by claiming to be above the kind of argument in which the laurel has been engaged, but then repeating such an argument in the birds' voices. The birds keep score on their own comparison of the trees as if it were a wrestling match (a 'fall' indicates the loser of each round). The discovery of the laurel was just the same as all the other trees; the olive was discovered by Athena, when she and Poseidon competed over Attica, with the snake-man Cecrops as the judge. So that round goes to the olive. Both are honoured by high-ranking gods: the crow sensibly calls that as a draw (this helps the olive to preserve a veneer of impartiality while really picking the ground for the contests in order to make sure that she wins). The olive is more useful (for people) than the laurel, providing *stemphylos* (a kind of olive-cake), oil (used for ointment) and the *kolymbas*, which consisted of olives in brine, but seems here to be taken as a drink (a 'dirty martini'?): this functions as a cross-reference within Callimachus' work to Theseus' reception by Hecale in her poem (cf. fr. 36 Hollis ~ 334, 248 Pfeiffer). The olive branch is held by suppliants, and that makes a third win for the olive; it is a surprise that the olive 'wins' a question about Delos, the island of Apollo, but Leto is supposed to have rested on an olive stump after the god's birth there. After the olive breaks off to comment on the birds' loquacity, the text is less well preserved but at the end the bird must be declaring that the laurel is defeated.

At this point, a third character enters the scene: the bramble. She tries to make peace by appealing to a 'team spirit' that should govern the relationship between the trees: it will delight their enemies to see them squabbling. The laurel, still angry, turns on her furiously: as far as she is concerned, the bramble is not 'one of us' with such noble trees as the laurel and olive, and she drives home her rejection of this idea with a string of oaths.

The two trees are characterized differently: the laurel is vainglorious and bad-tempered, while the olive is subtle and ironic. The olive wins. The poem is put together by a process of 'nesting' quoted speech; first the narrator, identified in the *diegesis* as the poet, is arguing with a rival, then he tells the story of the argument between the trees, interrupted by the bramble as Simos has interrupted his argument; within the argument between the laurel and the olive, the olive herself tells another fable-like story, presented as the argument she has herself heard between the two birds. Very clear patterns of resemblance between the 'frame' and the 'fable' of the trees are present but problematic and partial. Since the olive is the winner and presented as the cleverer of the two trees, it seems natural to see her as corresponding to the poet-narrator of the frame, and (according to the *diegesis*) it is the narrator who tells the fable of the trees, just as the olive reports the conversation of the two birds. Yet according to the *diegesis* it is the narrator who responds angrily to the attempted mediation by Simos, and this corresponds to the action of the laurel in the fable. It seems that Callimachus does not want us to be able to read across between the two stories too easily.

Both frame and fable contribute to the poem as a comedy of manners and status and exclusivity. What is the argument of the frame about? That the narrator calls Simos a 'Thracian' and 'boy-stealer' suggests an erotic context (Orpheus was said to have introduced pederasty to the Thracians, from whom it spread to other peoples). However, other features of the poem suggest a metapoetic context: that we are concerned with arguments at least partly to do with poetry. Interpreters have tended to suppose that the laurel and the olive somehow represent different poets or kinds of poetry. Thus Acosta-Hughes, rightly in my view, characterizes the dispute between the trees as a 'representation of a debate between different aesthetics, quite probably literary stylistics.'[7] He also points out that this *Iambus* seems to be very rich in reference to other poems by Callimachus. Thus Branchus (line 28) is the subject of a poem represented by fr. 229 Pfeiffer; the bringing of laurel branches to Delphi (34–6) was treated in the *Aetia* (frr. 86–9); most obviously, the dialogue between birds and the reference to Theseus drinking *kolymbas* at the house of Hecale (line 77; cf. *Hecale* fr. 36 Hollis ~ 334, 248 Pfeiffer) recall *Hecale*.[8] Again the poem seems to work more subtly than a straightforward identification of the olive with Callimachus and the laurel with his rival would allow: the trees are different in personality and style, but both are in some sense 'speaking Callimachus' (and it would be strange if the laurel were very straightforwardly the enemy of the poet, given the prominence of Apollo, whose tree it was, in Callimachus' other poetic pronouncements, as in the prologue to the *Aetia* and at the end of the *Hymn to Apollo*).

Conclusion

Callimachus' work is bursting with voices, from the human, animal and vegetable worlds and the world of inscription on stone. This variety is produced in a way which draws extensively on the poetry of the past. Epic poetry from Homer onwards is rich in speech and in the production of vividness through direct speech. In Attic drama we see in tragedy the poetry of enactment, and especially the poetry of highly emotional voices of mourning and emotion. Old comedy's delight in the ability of costume and acting, song and dance to make choruses of frogs, wasps, clouds and more stands in a family relationship with Callimachus' speaking trees and birds. Both draw on the ancient tradition of fables and of iambic poetry treating fable, as we see in the fragments of Archilochus (surviving fragments of Hipponax do not do this). Fascination with the ability of writing to make voices appear from objects is a part of the poetics of inscribed poetry in Greek from the very earliest times. Drawing on these precedents, Callimachus produces a poetry of multiple voices and speakers, at the same time as his poetry frequently refers to books and writing-tablets and the material quality of the written word: while Callimachus' poems were in all likelihood encountered both through performance and through reading, they encourage us to *think* of reading and writing, of the capacity of the material, written text to generate voices of all kinds, repeated and given new life in every act of reading.

Further reading

On fr. 64 and the world of inscriptions (and Simonides), see Rawles 2018b. *Hecale* is under-treated in recent scholarship, but Cameron 1995, 437–53 is helpful (and gives earlier bibliography), as is Fantuzzi and Hunter 2004, 191–200 and 249–55; Acosta-Hughes and Stephens 2012, 196–202 is suggestive on the Athenian quality of the poem and its relationship to tragedy. Acosta-Hughes 2002 gives extensive discussion of the *Iambi* and their relationship to earlier models.

3

Religion and the Gods

Introduction

In the treatment of religion and the gods, the tension between continuity and change in accounts of Callimachus and of Hellenistic literary culture comes to the fore. By some accounts, poetry of earlier times interacted with religion as a living force in communities, through being embedded in religious performance contexts as with tragedy and comedy, some performances of epic, and with lyric songs for performance at religious festivals such as paeans or dithyrambs. Hellenistic poetry, by this account, was composed in a different world where the age of the lyric poets is past and the religion of the old city states has been disrupted by political change, by the arrival of new gods, and by interaction between Greeks and their new non-Greek neighbours; its 'religious' content has more to do with scholarly connoisseurship of past poetic traditions than with 'real' or 'living' religion. Other treatments, however, have stressed elements of continuity in the world of religion and cult (and associated performance), and have sought to describe close connections between Callimachus, his poems and the world of contemporary religious practice.

There are, as I shall try to show, features of the texts which motivate both approaches; in what follows, I shall argue that, while Callimachean religion is strange and surprising, it should be read as 'serious' or 'real' engagement with religion, and far more than mere antiquarianism or literary 'playfulness'. I shall do this through a reading of parts of Callimachus' *Hymns*, though for reasons of space I shall treat them unevenly: most of what follows concerns the hymns to Apollo, Zeus and Delos, although what I say about the significance of singing and dancing choruses as important elements both in Callimachus' hymns and in contemporary religious experience could be applied to the *Hymn to Artemis* as well, while 'religious' readings of the last two hymns, especially the tragic and troubling *Bath of Pallas* (the fifth hymn, to Athena) have been explored in an important article by Richard Hunter.[1]

Background

We have seen (in the introduction) that the career of Alexander the Great and its aftermath radically transformed the Greek world, and that Alexandria in particular was a new city with a different relationship with the past from what we might find in, for example, Athens or Sparta or Argos. We can also see particular new or changed religious phenomena in Callimachus' world. For example, as we saw briefly when looking at voices (p. 47), this was a period in which living kings and queens could be worshipped as gods. The epigram beginning 'I am a conch …' (5 Pfeiffer = 14 Gow and Page) was dedicated to Arsinoë, who is also called by the name Cypris (i.e. Aphrodite): Arsinoë, the queen and sister of Ptolemy II, was worshipped as Aphrodite at a temple on the Egyptian coast at Zephyrium. In Egypt, this was a reflection of the way in which the Macedonian kings adopted the role, including the divine role, of the Pharaohs who had preceded them – but monarchs were treated as gods elsewhere too (Demetrius Poliorcetes was worshipped as a god in Athens, where he became king in 306 BC). This is a way in which religion was used to conceptualize a newly powerful kind of monarchy as much as a local peculiarity in Egypt. In Egypt, however, pre-existing religious structures were adopted in other ways as well. They were reflected in incestuous royal marriages, as of the *theoi adelphoi* ('sibling gods') Ptolemy II 'Philadelphus' and his sister Arsinoë: this was shocking by Greek standards, but sibling marriage was a Pharaonic tradition (Callimachus plays with the analogy of the siblings Zeus and Hera in his *Acontius and Cydippe*: see below, pp. 104–6). Other features of Egyptian religion were important in Ptolemaic Egypt and elsewhere: for example, the worship of Serapis, the Egyptian Osiris-Apis, was sponsored in Egypt by the Ptolemies but also spread elsewhere in the Greek (and later Roman) world. In many ways religious behaviour in Callimachus' world looked very different from the past.[2]

However, there was also much continuity. Ruler cult and the introduction of new gods supplemented but did not displace the worship of the gods and goddesses familiar already to Homer. In sanctuaries across the Greek world we can see the year-in-year-out operation of cult for the old gods continuing (from increasing numbers of inscriptions recording and regulating cult). This included musical performances and choruses. People sometimes used to speak of a 'lyric age' lasting until the mid-fifth century BC, the period from which most of our surviving lyric poetry comes.[3] As a way of describing the history of 'song culture' in the Greek world this is misleading. People worshipped the gods with singing and dancing choruses and other poetic and musical performances long after Pindar and long after Callimachus too.[4]

The intellectual world of Callimachus' day included unconventional opinions about religion. These lines, from the first *Iambus*, bring together different kinds of religious novelty (*Iambus* 1.9–11):

> Come, all together, to the temple outside the walls,
> where the old man who made up 'Long ago, Panchaean Zeus'
> scribbles his babblings in unjust books.

The speaker is the archaic iambic poet Hipponax, but he is addressing the contemporary intellectuals of the Museum, and his presence in their world is marked out by the temple, identified in an ancient synopsis of this poem as a temple of Serapis (Callimachus probably specified the place more precisely in a lost part of the poem). The old man whose work began 'Long ago, Panchaean Zeus' is Euhemerus of Messene, a contemporary of Callimachus whose work included a rationalizing account of religion by which the gods had originally been exceptional mortal humans, deified for their achievements. Yet even if this is symptomatic of an intellectual environment friendly to views which are hard to reconcile with traditional religion, it is not obvious that Callimachus is sympathetic to such views: at any rate the narrator, Hipponax, is hostile to Euhemerus' work.

Callimachus' *Hymns*

The question how remote Callimachus was from this world of religious continuity and performance is tricky, and we have little direct evidence; unsurprisingly, it presents itself most clearly in the book of six *Hymns*. Some of the *Hymns* at least *seem* to locate themselves in relation to traditional religious occasions and rituals, rather as some of the songs of earlier lyric poets like Pindar and Bacchylides do. However, it is unclear whether this reflects real performance contexts for the hymns. The collection is usually (and in my view correctly) seen to have been arranged as a meaningful sequence by Callimachus himself as the designer of his own book. This need not imply that they were first composed for literary arrangement; they might originally have belonged to different occasions and then have been ordered by the poet later on.

The *Hymns* also display Callimachus' learning and ingenuity, features of his work often seen as putting it in the world of the library rather than of public performances. Thus, for example, a perceptive reading of Callimachus' *Hymns* by Michael Haslam emphasizes ways in which they achieve meaning intertextually (especially but not only through interaction with the Homeric Hymns) and stresses wit, cleverness and the sense we may have of the poet as a presence in his own text.[5] For him, this contrasts with 'real' religion or religious meaning. In Haslam's reading of the *Hymn to Delos*, the Delian part of the Homeric Hymn to Apollo is described as 'something that is *there*, a constant presence behind the text, an icon with power (as distinct from the gods themselves, mere icons), liable at every moment to make its presence actively felt'.[6] At the end of his treatment, he concludes that 'The *Hymns*, it goes without saying, are literary texts. To call them religious is simply to say that they inscribe themselves within the genre. If we ask, Why Hymns?, the best answer might be, Why not? There was much mythological material about gods, and generically contextualizing it as hymnic had multiple poetic advantages over more straightforwardly narrative forms of presentation.'[7] This feels surprising. Our default assumption when dealing with antiquity should be that religion is 'real' religion and that gods are 'real' gods, not just a cast of poetic characters with stories attached. Yet it fitted into a tradition of reading Hellenistic poetry, and Callimachus in particular, as a very rarefied kind of poetry at a distance from the world. The features identified by Haslam are real, and he shows that his kind of reading 'works': but does this mean that these poems are *mere* literature, and not to be taken seriously as an engagement with religion?

Other approaches allow for different kinds of reading: readings which both show Callimachus' *Hymns* as more integrated in a wider world of religious practice and may involve serious consideration of performance in religious contexts.[8] Let us start with a poem already considered above (pp. 18–20): the *Hymn to Apollo*.

This, along with the *Hymn to Athena*, has been classified as a 'mimetic' hymn: it is written such that the narrator appears to be describing (and directing) the ritual events at a festival of Apollo as he speaks (lines 1–8):

> How it shook! – the sapling of Apollo's laurel!
> How the whole temple shook! Be off, be off, whoever is a sinner!
> And now Phoebus rattles the door with his beautiful foot.
> Can't you see? It nodded – the Delian palm nodded sweetly
> all of a sudden, and the swan sings beautifully high in the air.   5
> Bolts, swing away from the gates!
> Swing away, bars! The god is near at hand!
> And you, young men, prepare for the song and the dance!

The festival preparations are presented as a preparation for an epiphany of the god: and Apollo himself does appear and speak at the end of the poem, albeit not in quite the way we expect.

If this were a hymn from an earlier period, it would be assumed that it had been composed for performance in Cyrene (lines 65–71):

> It was also Phoebus who pointed out my fertile city to Battus   65
> and guided its people on their way into Libya in the form of a raven,
> at the founder's right hand, and swore that he would give battlements
> to our kings. And Apollo's oath always holds firm.
> Apollo, many call you Boedromios,
> and many Clarios, and everywhere your name is great.   70
> But I call you Carneios: this is my ancestral custom.

Battus was the legendary founder of Cyrene, and according to the custom of Cyrene the narrator calls Apollo by the cult title Carneius. The following lines explain how the cult title travelled from Sparta to the little island of Thera, from which Cyrene was founded, and thence to Cyrene itself; the poem continues to treat Apollo's special relationship with the city and its foundation up to line 96. On internal evidence it seems likely that the hymn was composed for a Cyrenean context; and regardless of its actual performance it is written such as to *seem* to relate to choral performance at Cyrene. Thus where the narrator refers to 'my king' this must mean 'the king of Cyrene' (probably Magas of Cyrene, who ruled *c.* 275–250 BC) (lines 25–7):[9]

It is bad to contend with the gods.
The man who fights the gods would fight my king.
The man who fights my king would fight even Apollo.

It is possible that part of the hymn represents a quoted 'choral' song, as the narrator leads us to expect that such a song is imminent in the first part of the hymn. If so, then passages with first person expressions (including the plural 'our kings' at 68) might represent the imagined voice of this chorus rather than the initial narrator.[10] However, at this point in the poem the narrator is still the speaker. Since Callimachus was from Cyrene, and since he makes this a part of the persona he projects elsewhere in his poems, it will have been easy for readers to identify this narrator with the historical poet. Likewise, the concluding part of the hymn, discussed above, reads as in part a statement of poetics, and this encourages a reading by which the poet himself is present in his text. The same association of Apollo with the projection of Callimachus' poetic persona can also be seen in the prologue to the *Aetia* (see above, pp. 28–40), where Apollo instructs the young Callimachus in poetry. It may be mapped on to what little can be told (or conjectured) about the historical poet as well as the persona projected in the poems: Apollo was, as the *Hymn to Apollo* shows, the special god of Cyrene, and it may be that the great altar of Apollo at Cyrene was rebuilt by Callimachus' great uncle, and thus that the cult was especially important in the history and self-perception of his own family.[11] In any case this hymn is composed in a way which 'chimes' with his self-representation in verse.

In formal terms, the usual way in which to describe Callimachean hymns such as this one is to focus on the interplay of two kinds of 'model'. One is the 'Homeric Hymns', the archaic hexameter poems in antiquity attributed to Homer with which Callimachus' hymns were transmitted. These were composed for solo rhapsodic performance at contests in the performance of epic poetry; early sources call them *prooimia* ('proems'), because they functioned as introductions before performances of epic poetry of the kind we know from the *Iliad* and *Odyssey*. Another model is the tradition of choral songs visible for us in, for example, the fragments of Pindar, for performance by choruses at religious festivals. Thus, while using the metre of the Homeric hymns and narrating myth about Apollo to explain his cult sites in a way which is similar to what some Homeric Hymns do, the voice of our hymn also evokes choral lyric by referring to choral performance (first at 8 above, where the narrator urges the chorus to get ready; again at 12–16, 28–31; 97–104 is an *aetion* for the ritual cry *hie paieon*, characteristic of the kind of choral song for Apollo called a *paean*; perhaps we should read quotation of the chorus' song beginning at 32, but the identity of the voice is uncertain). Yet while this account is (in my view) correct, it is also not the *only* way to describe the generic 'blend' of the hymn. References to choruses are not only a gesture towards the past, to a lost early classical world represented for Callimachus as for us by texts of Pindar and Bacchylides in the library; they are also a reference to continuing performance practice. Callimachus and his readers (or audiences!) have seen and in many cases participated in choruses; the presence of choral performance in this hymn is not only an archaicizing feature but also an appeal to contemporary religious experience. Through choral performances participants and audience form a community in relation to the divine, and this is religion, just as sacrifice or prayer is.

We can find the same 'double value' of other features of the poem which can be interpreted with a view to narrowly 'poetic' features and also with a view to interaction with religion and religious experience. The end of the hymn has frequently, as above (pp. 18–20), been read as a statement of poetics (105–13):

Envy spoke secretly in Apollo's ear:
'I do not admire the singer who sings not as much as the sea.'
Apollo kicked Envy and spoke as follows:

'The stream of the Assyrian river is big, but it drags along
many scourings from the land and much rubbish on its water.
To Deo the Melissae do not bring water from everywhere,
but the little stream that comes up pure and undefiled
from a holy spring, the choicest essence.'
Farewell, Lord! As for Blame, let him go where Envy dwells!

That poetry is a large point of what these lines are 'about' is clear: ἀοιδός (*aoidos*), 'singer', is an archaicizing word for 'poet'. Apollo endorses a poetic aesthetic of smallness and purity, favouring the little, pure spring rather than the large and dirty river Euphrates. Yet this is not only about aesthetics. Ivana Petrovic has shown that this part of the poem and others are closely related to the contemporary religious phenomenon of inscriptions regulating ritual practice at cult sites: the participants must be good, pure, virtuous, and the sacrifices likewise.[12] We have an inscription (late fourth century BC) specifying the ritual purity required for cult observances in Cyrene, such as the festival of Apollo that this poem describes. It presents itself as an oracular response from Apollo, beginning as follows:[13]

Apollo issued an oracle: The Cyrenaeans shall inhabit Libya for ever, observing purifications and abstinences and tithes.

The word for 'purification' is κάθαρμα (*katharma*), closely related to the adjective καθαρός (*katharos*), 'pure', as used in the hymn. Apollo's instructions for the 'right kind' of poetry in the hymn resemble the instructions he gives in the Cyrenean purity regulations: the poet must bring to Apollo the right kind of song, as the Melissae (priestesses of Demeter = Deo) bring to her the right kind of water and a worshipper must make the right kind of sacrifice.

If we focus on the end of the poem as 'purely' about poetics, then other features may be read in the same light. These lines (9–11) might enhance a sense that Callimachus' hymn is 'exclusive' poetry, for the elite and educated reader (especially when we realize that the eventual 'epiphany' is the lines from the end of the poem quoted above: perhaps Apollo's advice about small-scale poetry is advice that only an elite will understand):

> Apollo does not show himself to everybody, but only to whoever is good.
> Whoever sees him, this man is great; whoever does not, that man is lowly.
> We shall see you, Far-worker, and we shall not at all be lowly.

However, this language can also be paralleled from contemporary cult and the inscriptional record, where inscriptions proclaim that only the pure of heart, or only the good, may enter the sanctuary (cf. 'Be off, be off, whoever is a sinner!' in line 2).[14] Even the idea that the content of a hymn is sanctioned or mandated by Apollo himself can be paralleled from hymns and inscriptions clearly connected with real ritual practice.[15]

In short, this hymn, often read as a document of aesthetics, showing us how Callimachus sets out his ideas about poetry and distinguishes himself from predecessors and contemporaries, can also be read as a poem which consistently relates closely to contemporary religion and cult practice, in a way which seems to reflect the poet-narrator's own identity as a Cyrenean of a family particularly associated with that city's cult of Apollo and religious identity. We need not choose between these options. Apollo is, after all, a god particularly associated with poetry; it is appropriate for a hymn to Apollo to be concerned with poetry. As we have already seen (above, p. 18), the sudden end to the hymn functions in part as a resolution of a problem both religious and poetic raised earlier (28–31):

> Apollo will honour that chorus, which sings according to his liking.
> He has the power: he sits at the right hand of Zeus.
> Nor will a chorus sing of Apollo for only one day.
> For he is rich in song; who would not easily sing of Apollo?

This raises the question: how long will the song be? If it is to match Apollo's greatness and the wealth of themes his achievements and qualities provide, it seems it might go on forever. This is both a poetic and a religious problem: the question 'how long should a song be?' maps closely on to the question 'how can a song match up to the divine theme of Apollo?' The answer is that a song should not try to match in length the importance and richness of its subject matter: the challenge of making a song *big* enough to match Apollo as a theme is declined. Singing according to Apollo's taste has a different meaning: he likes what is small and pure and perfect, and the questions of religion and poetics fuse together in his epiphany and endorsement of the song.

The *Hymn to Apollo* is the second place (if we read the book of *Hymns* in order) where we encounter this 'how long?' question. The hymns exhibit an inverse relationship between 'bigness' of subject matter and 'bigness' of poem. The first poem, and shortest, is the *Hymn to Zeus*, the greatest god; the second, and second shortest, is the *Hymn to Apollo*, a particularly important god for the poet-narrator and within Callimachus' works. Conversely, the middle two hymns are longer, and that for the tiny island of Delos is longest of all. In the first hymn of the set, the *Hymn to Zeus*, we see reasons why this poetry has been seen as not really 'religious' by the kind of reading exemplified by the essay by Michael Haslam quoted above (lines 1–9):

> Zeus – is anything better to sing alongside libations
> than the god himself, always great, always the lord,
> who put the Pelagonians to flight and gave justice to the Ouranidae?
> And how shall we sing of him? As Dictaean, or Lykaian?
> My heart is split two ways, since his birth is disputed.   5
> Zeus, some say you were born on the mountains of Ida;
> Zeus, some say in Arcadia. Which, father, are lying?
> 'Cretans are always liars!' Indeed: the Cretans even
> fabricated a tomb for you. But you did not die; you are forever.

Unlike the *Hymn to Apollo*, this hymn does not locate itself at a festival with choral performance but at a sympotic gathering where libations (offerings of wine) are to be made (it is not usually classified as 'mimetic': but the opening lines *suggest* concurrent activities, in this case drinking and libation). The narrator's problem, however, seems close to the scholarly poet's: how to decide between rival traditions? Specifically, how to deal with the problem that both Mt Ida (on Crete) and Dicte (in Arcadia) claimed to be the birthplace of Zeus? Zeus' reply seems frivolous: 'Cretans are always liars!' (Cretans were proverbially deceitful in antiquity, and the phrase was the source of a logical paradox: if a Cretan says 'Cretans are always liars', is he telling the truth or lying?). Yet the narrator's response to this seems more serious: a local tradition involving a 'tomb of Zeus', such as the Cretans pointed to, seems incompatible with a 'proper' theology of Zeus as an eternal and divine being. The story of the god's birth that follows combines Arcadian and Cretan episodes, and occupies most of the poem. It concludes with Zeus on the cusp of adulthood, and another place where the poet-narrator overtly confronts traditions from the past and whether or not to endorse them (lines 55–65):

> You grew well, you were raised well, heavenly Zeus;   55
> quick as a flash you shot up, and your first beard grew thick
>   and fast.
> But while you were still a child, you thought everything through
>   to the end.
> Wherefore your brothers, older though they were,
> did not begrudge that you had heaven for your allotted home –
> but the ancient poets were altogether untruthful!   60
> They said that the lot decided the homes for Kronos' sons three
>   ways.
> But who would draw lots for both Olympus and Hades,
> unless a real ninny? A lottery is for equal shares:
> these are as different as can be!
> May *my* lies persuade my listener's ears!   65

Again the narrator confronts the question whether to accept or reject stories from the past, this time specifically from poets from the past. Most famously at *Iliad* 15.187–93, the division of zones of power between the three brothers, Poseidon, Hades and Zeus, was decided by lot. Differently, in Hesiod's *Theogony* (881–5), the gods invited Zeus to rule over them after the defeat of the Titans, and he assigned their areas of responsibility to them. Callimachus prefers something like the second version: he goes on to say that it was through great deeds and power that Zeus achieved his position. Yet the way in which he gets there is strange. Rather than simply accepting the Hesiodic version he makes a display of rejecting the Homeric alternative; and he does so by an odd kind of rationalizing. It does not make sense, he says, to draw lots as a way of deciding between prizes of unequal value. Yet it is not obvious why this should be true: *why not* draw lots to decide who will get the best prize, who the second best, and who the third?[16] When he goes on to appeal to the importance of plausibility ('May *my* lies persuade my listeners' ears!'), evoking a tradition associating plausible lies, poetry and fiction that goes back to Hesiod (*Theogony* 27), it seems to invite the question '*Why* is this version more plausible?', and the answer is not necessarily obvious. Again Callimachus dramatizes his own poetic choices, presented as something of a mystery and motivated as much by concern for plausibility as for truth.

As the poem continues the analogy developed between Zeus and the king Ptolemy provides a different reason to emphasize that Zeus' power derives from his own strength. The poet quotes Hesiod, 'Kings are from Zeus' (line 79: cf. Hesiod, *Theogony* 96) and from the theme of Zeus' special association with kingship moves to praise of Ptolemy before stopping rather abruptly (lines 84–96: the end of the poem):

> You cast floods of wealth upon them [*i.e., kings*] and riches in plenty –
> for all of them, but not for all equally. This can clearly be judged   85
> from the case of our king: for he steps far beyond the rest.

In the evening he accomplishes what he thought of in the morning
(the biggest things in the evening; smaller things as soon as he
thinks them).
Others accomplish their purposes in a year; others not even then.
For others again,
You curtail their plans' fulfilment yourself, and cut short their
desire.   90
Hail, Lord most high, Kronos' son, giver of good things,
giver of safety. Who will sing your deeds?
Nobody has, and nobody will: who could sing the deeds of Zeus?
Hail, father, hail once more. Give virtue and wealth!
Without virtue wealth knows not how to profit men;   95
nor without wealth virtue. Give both virtue and riches!

So the poem describes Zeus' birth, briefly treats his progress to adulthood, the division of responsibility between Zeus and his two brothers, and describes his association with kingship in such a way as to praise Ptolemy (Ptolemy II, like Zeus a younger brother with more power than his older brothers), and then stops abruptly, with the ending being prompted by the question, 'Who will sing your deeds? [...] Who could sing the deeds of Zeus?' This is similar to the situation in the *Hymn to Apollo*, where the final epiphany of the god cuts short the poem and thus resolves the question invited at lines 30-1: if a chorus could sing for more than a whole day about Apollo, how can the song come to an end? The device motivates the end of the poem, and we must suppose that Zeus' deeds are in fact either too big or too numerous to be sung. Part of the reason why the answer to the question 'Who will sing your deeds?' is 'Nobody' may be to do with the lack of any substantial Homeric Hymn to Zeus (but of course there are hymns to Zeus elsewhere in literary tradition: e.g. Aeschylus *Agamemnon* 355-474, *Suppliant Women* 524-99).[17]

The end of the hymn invites a larger question, here as in the *Hymn to Apollo* as much religious as literary: what *would* constitute a proper telling of Zeus' deeds and greatness? Perhaps Zeus is so great and so 'high' that it is beyond human ability to grasp his greatness and to treat it fittingly: any attempt to produce sublimity to match Zeus' power is side-stepped as impossible and/or as something which Callimachus' aesthetic does not encourage him to try.[18] The refusal to move from Zeus' early years to an attempt to 'capture' the god more fully by narrating his deeds and producing a longer poem may be interpreted as a confrontation of a serious problem of religion: how can a human 'capture' Zeus?

One consequence of the side-stepping of Zeus' great deeds is that the emphasis of the poem is largely on his childhood: the narrative treatment of the god stops when he grows his first beard. The effect of emphasis on birth and childhood is to provoke reflection on the asymmetry of divine lives by comparison with human lives. Gods may be eternal in the sense that they are undying, but since their mythology involves their parents and birth they are not without a beginning: there was a time before Zeus. The first lines of the hymn are especially telling here: the poet is judging between alternative stories of Zeus' birthplace, but rejects the Cretans' story on the grounds that they claim also to have his tomb: 'But you did not die; you are forever.'

The same emphasis on birth and childhood is characteristic of the central two hymns, to Artemis and (the longest hymn for the tiny island) to Delos, birthplace of Apollo. It is to the second of these that I now turn. In its focus on female experience and choruses of women and girls, the *Hymn to Delos* forms a sequel to the *Hymn to Artemis*; but in a different way it forms a pair to the *Hymn to Apollo*, since for both the main model is the *Homeric Hymn to Apollo*, which has two parts, the first part concerning Apollo and Delphi and the other, as here, concerning Apollo and Delos, the god's birthplace. Some of the most distinctive features of this hymn are visible from the beginning (lines 1–27):

> Oh, my heart – for how long, and when, will you sing of
> Delos, Apollo's nurse? Truly all the
> Cyclades, holiest of the islands that lie in the sea,

are rich in song. But Delos demands the first prize
from the Muses, since she washed and swaddled 5
Phoebus, whose care is for songs, and first praised him as a god.
Just as the Muses hate the poet who does not sing of
Pimpleia, so Phoebus hates whoever forgets Delos.
Now I shall give a share of song to Delos, so that Apollo
Cynthius may praise me, because I respected his dear nurse. 10
She – she is windswept, unploughed and sea-beaten,
a course for seagulls more than for horses –
she is fixed in the sea, and the great sea, whirling,
wipes away much foam from the Icarian water.
And so it was that sea-faring fishermen settled on her. 15
Yet none begrudge that she is named in first place,
whenever to the house of Ocean and the Titan Tethys
the islands throng, and she always leads the group.
Behind her Phoenician Cyrnos follows in her footsteps
(no unworthy island herself!), and Abantian Macris of the
    Ellopians, 20
and lovely Sardinia, and the island to which Cypris swam
out of the sea for the first time, and for this she protects it.
These are fortified by ramparts circling round them,
Delos by Apollo. What barrier could be stronger?
Walls and stones may fall under the blast 25
of Strymonian Boreas, but a god is a permanent protection.
Beloved Delos, such is the support around you.

The premise of the poem is that the little island of Delos is also an anthropomorphic goddess; and indeed islands as also rivers and various other parts of the ancient landscape are often so treated (cities as well: Callimachus' Cyrene was also the name of a nymph, beloved of Apollo). Here the islands are personified to the extent that they can form a group and process in order to visit Ocean and his wife Tethys, and Delos takes the lead (the word used, ἔξαρχος, *exarchos*, 'leader', line 18, is one which could be used of the leader of a chorus, and choruses are a recurring theme in the poem). The island of Delos was, since the sixth century, a major multi-polis cult site for the worship of Apollo, who was born there to his mother Leto, and the birth of Apollo is the island's great achievement in Callimachus' poem. It was at this point, we are told, that Delos stopped being a mobile, floating island and put down 'the roots of your feet' (line 54). Now Delos is 'fixed in the sea' (line 13) – except that, by the conceit of treating the islands as deities with human features, it seems that she can *also* lead a chorus of islands to their parents' house. This tension between the mobile and the static runs through the poem, alongside the choral theme, and co-exists with a contrast between circular and linear motion.[19] Immediately after the lines quoted above, the narrator addresses the island (lines 28–9):

> Since a very great many songs run around you,
> into what shall I weave you? What is it your pleasure to hear?

The image of songs running around the island suggests the motion of a circular chorus. However, the topic with which the narrator begins is the former mobility of Delos, before she acquired that name, and involves a different kind of motion (lines 36–40):

> your name was
> Asteria of old, when you leapt into the sea's great trench
> from heaven, fleeing marriage with Zeus, like a shooting-star.
> For as long as golden Leto did not mix with you,
> For so long you were still called Asteria, and not yet Delos.

Asteria's motion into the sea was the straight-line movement of a shooting-star (the word for star, ἀστέρι, *asteri*, explains the name: this was not, then, her *original* name, but before Zeus attempted to seduce her, she was called something else), and in the lines which follow her wandering is described, as she moves between different parts of the Aegean apparently at random. This is then followed by the longest section of the poem, describing the wanderings of Leto, impregnated by Zeus and looking for somewhere to give birth. All places refuse her, because they are afraid of punishment by Hera, who is angry because of Zeus' infidelity and has stationed Ares and Iris as lookouts to spot any place giving Leto shelter. However, where I write that they 'refuse her' I am quietly rationalizing, since Callimachus' text is more startling (lines 70–85):

> Arcadia fled; the holy mountain of Auge fled,   70
> Parthenion; old man Pheneios fled behind;
> the whole of Pelops' land, adjoining the Isthmus, fled,
> except for Aegialos, that is, and Argos. For her these paths
> were untrodden, since Inachos belongs to Hera.
> By the same route fled Aonia; Dirke and Strophie   75
> followed, holding the hand of their father
> black-pebbled Ismenos, and Asopos, heavy-kneed,
> followed far behind, struck by a thunderbolt.
> And the nymph stopped whirling in the dance,
> Melie, born from the earth, and her cheek turned pale   80
> as she gasped for her age-mate the oak tree, when she saw
> Helicon's hair shaken. Muses, goddesses, tell me:
> is it true that the oaks are the same age as the Nymphs?
> 'The Nymphs rejoice, when the rain makes grow the oaks.
> The Nymphs lament, when the leaves fall from the oaks.'   85

Arcadia, Parthenion, Pheneios, the land of Pelops (probably the Argolid is intended rather than the whole Peloponnese), Aegialos, Argos, Aonia, Dirke, Strophie, Ismenos, Asopos: these are all areas, mountains, rivers, all presented as living, moving creatures just like Asteria herself, whose mobility is no longer unique in this strange and chaotic world where the fixed points of Greek geography can run away in fear of Hera's anger. The places are halfway between geography and divinity, as we can see with the Theban river Ismenos, which (who!) can have his daughters hold his hand, but is still described as 'black-pebbled'.

The narrator at this point, rather like the scholarly narrator of the *Aetia*, suddenly breaks off to ask a question of the Muses. Yet the meaning of the question (and its answer) is obscure, and its relevance to the poem is hard to define precisely. In its immediate context it seems to be prompted by the anxiety of Melie, the nymph of the *ash* tree, who shares its name, about the *oaks* of Helicon.[20] This somehow reminds the narrator of a question: are oak trees the same age as nymphs? Probably we should understand this as meaning something like, 'do the nymphs come into being, grow up, and die simultaneously with the trees for which they are named?' This is what some (but not all) ancient sources say, i.e. that for each tree there is a nymph which shares its life-cycle (see, for example, *Homeric Hymn to Aphrodite* 264–72); other sources have nymphs living far longer than trees.[21] The response (do the Muses speak, lines 84–5?) is unclear; it asserts the nymphs' close emotional connection with the oaks rather than confirming or denying the synchronization of their life-cycles. The sense of emotion, nature and the sacred intertwined seems as close as Callimachus gets to the world of Theocritus' bucolic poems, but the lines are hard to interpret as an answer to the narrator's question. What is at stake seems to be closely related to the question prompted by this whole section of the poem: are the divinities corresponding to places, rivers, mountains, trees and so on *identical with* those features of the landscape, or do they merely somehow *stand for* them? Is the god Ismenus both so anthropomorphic that it has hands and daughters and so closely identical with the river that when the god refuses Leto the river itself moves away from her? This is a central question in a hymn addressed to a goddess who is also an island. As previously in Callimachus' hymns, we find ourselves at a place where there is a delicate tension between 'religious' and 'poetic' questions: what we might call an extended poetic metaphor or 'conceit' (the islands run away from Leto's approach) overlaps with a question about how to conceive of ancient religious traditions about the sacred landscape, in which rivers are (or 'have' – this is the question!) gods, trees and cities are (or have?) nymphs, and so on.

In this part of the poem the movement thematized is a zigzag one by which Leto turns first to one place and then another, while the places themselves shrink away from her. As the poem continues, this movement is broken up by three big set-pieces. First (lines 86–99), the god Apollo, still in Leto's womb, addresses Thebe, nymph of Thebes, who also refuses a place for Leto to give birth. The unborn god angrily prophesies of how he and Artemis will kill the children of Niobe at Thebes. The theme of divine childhood visible in Callimachus' *Hymn to Artemis* and the *Homeric Hymn to Hermes* is here taken to a new extreme: Apollo is divine and precocious even before his birth. Second (lines 103–52), Leto implores the river Peneius, in Thessaly, to receive her, and he initially agrees; but seeing Ares preparing to punish him Leto changes her mind and tells Peneius to save himself and then moves from the mainland of Greece to the islands. The third set-piece is another prophecy of Apollo from the womb (lines 160–95: see below, pp. 96–8): the god tells his mother not to give birth on the island of Cos, which is to be held back for another birth, the birth of Ptolemy (he means Ptolemy II 'Philadelphus'), predicts Ptolemy's defeat of the Gaulish attackers at Delphi (this happened in 279 BC), and instructs her to find the mobile island Asterie ('but', thinks the reader, 'in this world *everything* seems to be mobile!').

Leto gives birth on Asterie, and when she is informed on Olympus Hera, though angry, forgives Asterie on the grounds that she had jumped into the sea rather than consenting to adultery with Zeus: here we see the end of Hera's speech and the passage following (lines 247–59):

> ... But I honour her [*sc. Asterie*] to an astonishing degree, since she did not trample my bed, but chose the sea rather than Zeus.
>
> So she spoke, and swans, singers of the god about to be born,
> leaving Maeonian Pactolus behind, circled   250
> seven times around Delos and sang for the birth,

birds of the Muses, most songful of birds
(from this the child attached the same number of lyre-strings
later: the same as the number of times the swans sang at his birth).
They did not sing an eighth time: the god leapt up, and with
  resounding voice
the Delian nymphs, offspring of the ancient river,   256
pronounced the holy song of Eileithuia. At once
the brazen sky echoed to the piercing cry!

Nor did Hera keep her resentment, since Zeus removed her anger.

C-major chorus! We return to circular movement as the singing swans circle the island, before making way for the chorus of Deliades singing the song of Eileithuia, goddess of childbirth. Hera's anger disappears; all is right with the world. The musical emphasis is brought out by the reference to Apollo's future invention of the lyre. As the hymn continues, the emphasis is on wealth and beauty and praise of Delos, and again the new order, civilized and stable, is characterized by choruses. In lines 279–99 we see various people sending choruses to Delos. Here the island is the destination of centripetal motion as the choruses gather; this replaces the zigzag dashing about of the wandering sections. Again we also see the island's own chorus of Deliades: the 'Delian nymphs' named in 256 (above) are, in historical times, a real chorus of mortal 'Delian maidens' (296–8: these are also mentioned as a famous chorus at *Homeric Hymn to Apollo* 156–64). The choral significance of the island comes through even more strongly in the lines which follow, where the significance of the island as a centre of choral activity is set into the mythological past (lines 300–15):

Fragrant Asterie! Round and around you the islands   300
made a circle and surrounded you as a chorus.
Shaggy-haired Hesperos was neither silent nor noiseless,
but always he looks down on you with shouting all around.

> The people listen to the tune of the ancient Lycian
> which the seer Olen brought from the Xanthos. 305
> The girls of the chorus beat the solid ground with their feet.
> At this point the sacred image is weighed down with garlands,
> the celebrated image of ancient Cypris, which Theseus once
> dedicated alongside the youths when he sailed from Crete.
> These, Mistress, fleeing the roar of the fierce son 310
> of Pasiphae and the twisted corners of the labyrinth,
> having gathered for a purification around your sacred altar,
> danced in a circle, and Theseus led the chorus.
> From that day on, as immortal offerings from their pilgrimage,
> Cecrops' sons send to Phoebus the rigging of that ship. 315

Circles and choruses; choruses and circles. The islands called the Cyclades (the name comes from κύκλος, *kyklos*, 'circle') are figured as a chorus dancing around with Delos in the centre. The linear chorus of islands which Delos leads to visit Ocean and Tethys at the beginning of the poem is here complemented by a circular chorus of islands with Delos at its centre (this feels like a change over time; but the opening lines describe the present situation of Delos, so the sense we might look for, that linear movement is replaced over time by circular movement, cannot be right – the present island can be associated with both). Delos is also the centre of human choruses, which dance in circular motion by night while Hesperos, the evening star, looks on. Is he 'shaggy' as another way of bringing out a tension between things in the world of nature and their anthropomorphized divine counterparts? Perhaps Hesperos could be depicted as a man with shaggy hair – yet the star itself is not shaggy . . .[22]

Just as Delos has a story explaining how it came to be in the middle of its chorus of islands, so the human choruses have a history also. A traditional cult song at Delos was believed to have been brought there from the east by a Lycian seer, Olen; the ancient statue of Aphrodite was dedicated by Theseus when he came to Delos with the Athenian youths whom he rescued from Crete with Ariadne's help. They too danced in a circle, and the circle contrasts with the twisting shapes of the labyrinth; the Athenians dedicate the rigging of his ship at Delos even now (the Athenians claimed that the ship that carried their delegation to Apollo's festival at Delos was the same in which Theseus had sailed).[23] Finally, we arrive at the present day and the continuity of worship and of choral performance, with its roots reaching back into the mythical past, but extending into the present experience of Callimachus and his audience, who may themselves have seen or participated in choral performances on Delos and will in any case have experienced choral performance elsewhere as part of their religious lives. Within the world of the hymn, chorality and circular choral movement stand for order; the ordered circular motion of choruses replaces the chaotic zigzagging of Asteria's and Leto's wanderings that comes to an end with the birth of the musical god, Apollo. This can clearly be seen as a religious conception, despite the multiple playfulnesses and weirdnesses of the poem's treatment of myth and movement. We end with perhaps the strangest passage of all (lines 316–26):

> Asteria, of many altars and many prayers, what merchant
> sailor of the Aegean has passed you by on his swift ship?
> Winds so great do not blow him,
> nor necessity drive the ship as quickly as possible, but the sailors
> quickly furled the sails, and did not again embark   320
> before whirling around your altar, buffeted
> with blows, and biting the sacred stump of the olive
> with hands tied behind their backs. The Delian nymph invented these
> as amusing games for the growing child Apollo.
> Oh well-hearthed one, hearth of the islands, hail to you!   325
> And hail to Apollo, and his sister that Leto bore!

Key themes are reprised in bizarrely altered form. Delos as hearth is a new metaphor to express the same idea as the chorus of islands, Delos as the centre of a circle; but she also has many hearths, since many sacrifices are made there. The sailor, like Leto, stops his journey at Delos (but now the island is already fixed in place when he passes). The circular movement of choruses is reprised in the bizarre ritual by which the sailors circle the altar while striking it (or possibly while themselves being struck – scholars have suggested emendation to try to make sense of this passage) and bite the olive stump with their hands behind their backs. These strange rituals, though unattested elsewhere, are unlikely to be a Callimachean invention: but how to explain them? Again we are reminded of Callimachus the writer of *aetia*, as at the very end of the poem he explains these practices as games taught to Apollo by a nymph of the island (unless 'Delian nymph' refers to the island herself).

To the very end, then, the *Hymn to Delos* excels in defamiliarization and weirdness. As often in Callimachus, we can sense the 'scholarly' aetiologizing poet behind the narrator. Traditional ideas (the mobile island is already seen in Pindar) are taken to bizarre extremes, as is Callimachus' interest in the early childhood of gods (also traditional in hymns). It is also in various ways a very 'human' story. We feel for Leto especially in her exhaustion and victimhood at the hands of Hera.[24] Its main movement is from chaos to order, expressed above all in the contrast of shapes and movements which I have explored above, which expresses in particular the establishment of a kind of order associated with the chorus: an apt way in which to hymn a musical god, and one which chimes not only with a history of choral performance and choral poetry of the past, but with the lived religious experience of Callimachus' own time.

Conclusions

We do not know whether Callimachus' hymns were composed for performance in a context related to the rituals they frequently describe, though we should not rule out such a connection. They indisputably show the spirit of the Hellenistic age as it has traditionally been perceived in Callimachus' work: they are rich in significant interaction with the poetry of the past, they feature a prominent and 'scholarly' narrator, they are witty, clever, and frequently strange in a way which seems to involve a degree of alienation and distance on the part of the reader. They repay the kind of reading strategy instantiated by the article from Michael Haslam that I quoted close to the beginning of this chapter: a reading focusing on clever, ironized, hyper-literary writing and play with the poetry of the past. And yet ... Callimachus' hymns can also be read, as I have tried to illustrate here, in a way which emphasizes different features. They repeatedly engage with the world of performance, cult and ritual – and this is not merely an antiquarian feature but also an interaction with living religion in the world of Callimachus and his audience. Their form relates them not only to past models but to contemporary worship, even if the world of cult is transposed into a different and characteristically Callimachean 'key'.

We should be wary of accepting a contrast between ironized, playful sophistication on one hand and 'real' religion on the other (the analogy is highly restricted – Greek does not have 'devotional poetry' of intimate, personal religiosity in the same way as the Christian tradition – but the example of English poets from Donne to Eliot should make us cautious about any such contrast), just as our instinct should be to resist any interpretation of an ancient text by which religion and the gods are merely decorative and 'literature' itself is the only point. Whether or not this is a poetry of intense personal commitment to religion (we may doubt the appropriateness of this kind of language for describing poetic religion in antiquity tout court – I make no claim to know how 'pious' or 'devout' the historical Callimachus was, though we should not assume that he was not), it is a poetry which engages with the religious sphere, with the meanings of divinity and of worship, in a way which shows strong elements of continuity with the poetry of the past.

Further reading

Stephens 2015 is an excellent guide to the *Hymns* and can be used (selectively) by the Greekless. Cameron 1995, chapter 2 discusses possible performance contexts for Callimachus' poems. Hunter 1992 is an important discussion, which he takes up again in Hunter 2011. Bulloch 1984 is a perceptive reading stressing responses to cultural change. Petrovic 2011 is very good on connections between the *Hymn to Apollo* and contemporary religion as visible in the inscriptions.

4

People and Places

In the previous chapter, we saw many places in the book of *Hymns* where the poetry gives a prominent place to geography (most spectacularly in the *Hymn to Delos*), and makes space for material concerning contemporary kings ('my king' at *Hymn to Apollo* 26–7, the prophecy concerning Ptolemy II at *Hymn to Delos* 162–95, praise of the same Ptolemy at *Hymn to Zeus* 79–90). These, Callimachus' treatment of contemporary people and places in the political world of the third century BC, are the closely related topics of this chapter. We have seen already in the introduction that the world of Callimachus was one in which both geography and politics had in important ways been reconfigured in the generation before Callimachus' activity, with the rise of big military monarchies such as the Ptolemaic dynasty at Alexandria, and the expansion of the Greek world southwards into Egypt and eastwards in Asia. Reflections of these new phenomena in Callimachus' poems (and their relationship with much older traditions) are explored here.

Geography and colonization: Cyrene and the *Hymn to Apollo*

In the *Hymn to Apollo* the narrator identifies himself as a Cyrenean and describes that city's relationship with Apollo and his festival of the Carneia (lines 65–79):

> It was also Phoebus who pointed out my fertile city to Battus   65
> and guided its people on their way into Libya in the form of a raven,

at the founder's right hand, and swore that he would give battlements
to our kings. And Apollo's oath always holds firm.
Apollo, many call you Boedromios,
and many Clarios, and everywhere your name is great.   70
But I call you Carneios: this is my ancestral custom.
Sparta, Carneios, was your first shrine;
second was Thera, and the town of Cyrene was third.
For it was out of Sparta that the sixth generation of Oedipus' line
led you to their foundation on Thera; and it was out of Thera   75
that ominous Aristoteles established you in the land of the
    Asbystians.
He built for you a very fine palace, and in the city
he set up annual rituals in which for the last time
many bulls fall to their knees, my Lord.

Here the narrator explains the involvement of Apollo in the foundation of the city, and this is closely tied to the celebration of the Carneia festival, which moves along with the colonizers, first from Sparta to the little island of Thera, in the southern Aegean, and then from Thera to Libya, led by Aristoteles, also known by the nickname Battus. This colonization story must have been hard-wired into the collective memory of Cyrene: it is for us one of the best attested colonization narratives to have survived out of archaic Greece (the traditional date for the foundation of the colony is 631 BC). Herodotus preserves different versions of the story (4.147–58: the different communities in Sparta, Thera and Cyrene have different accounts), and each of three songs by Pindar commemorating victors from Cyrene in the pan-Hellenic games gives a different myth-historical account of Cyrene's origins and links with 'old' Greece. The enormous *Pythian* 4 ties the mythical pre-history of Cyrene into the voyage of Argo, and also mentions the colonization by Battus; in *Pythian* 5 we hear again of Battus but also of the earlier history of the Spartans as descendants of Heracles and the movement from Sparta to Thera to Cyrene; *Pythian* 9 tells how Apollo encountered and fell in love with the nymph Cyrene in Thessaly, and took her to Libya where they were married by Aphrodite.¹ Callimachus is thus working in a long established tradition of affirming the Hellenic identity of Cyrene and its relationship with a much older world of Greeks in the Aegean and in peninsular Greece.

This is a part of a broader phenomenon by which Greeks in the archaic period used myth-historical stories to explain the relationship between communities in time and space, both as here as ways of placing colonies in relation to older cities and also as a way of presenting the relationships between Greeks and the other peoples in the expanding world they inhabited. In an example to which we will return, Io, the daughter of Inachus, as a result of the erotic attentions of Zeus was transformed by Hera into a cow and pursued by a gadfly to Egypt, where she gave birth to Zeus' son Epaphus. Epaphus was then the ancestor of Libya (from whom are descended the Libyans) and of Aegyptus (Mr Egypt) and his brother Danaus. Here the story becomes more complicated: Danaus and his fifty daughters reverse Io's journey and come to Argos, ruled by Pelasgus, and are eventually received into the city and married to Argive husbands. The Greeks believed that much of peninsular Greece had been in prehistory inhabited by the Pelasgians, while 'Danaans' is one of the terms that describes 'Greeks' in early poetry: the repeated use of ethnic names as personal names means that the function of this mythical material in describing ethnic history and identity is very transparent. We first see extensive treatment of this material in Aeschylus' *Suppliant Women* and the *Prometheus Bound* attributed to the same poet; but the origin of the myths is much older, going back at least to the seventh century BC.² This kind of mythology about the relationship between places and peoples through time and space is available for Hellenistic poets to draw on and modify as they engage with the enlarged and transformed Greek world of the third century.

With Cyrene, Callimachus' treatment of the Carneia as a festival symbolizing the colony's identity and links with Sparta and Thera is already suggested in Pindar (*Pythian* 5.72–85), in a poem which may itself have been composed for performance at the festival. The story of Apollo's marriage to Cyrene, as found in Pindar's *Pythian* 9 (lines 85–96), is blended by Callimachus into the description of the Carneia:

> Truly Phoebus rejoiced greatly, when the men in their
>   war-belts   85
> danced with the fair-haired Libyan women,
> when for them the appointed Carneian time arrived.
> The Dorians were not yet able to approach the springs of Cyre,
> but they inhabited Azilis, rich in wooded vales.
> The lord himself looked upon them, and showed them to his
>   bride   90
> while he stood on Myrtoussa, the horn-shaped mountain,
>   where the daughter
> of Hypseus slew the lion that plundered Eurypylus' cattle.
> Apollo saw no chorus more godly than that one,
> nor did he give such benefactions to any city as much as to Cyrene,
> remembering his first abduction of her. Nor did they,   95
> Battus' descendants, honour any other god more than Phoebus.

Here he presents the first settlers from Thera (all male) celebrating the first Carneia to be held in Cyrene by dancing with women from the pre-Greek population. At this point they have not yet founded the city itself (the spring Cyre was used in etymologizing its name, but the alternative was to derive it from the name of the nymph Cyrene, Apollo's bride and the daughter of Hypseus: Callimachus is having it both ways). First they live in the Libyan region of Azilis (called Aziris in Herodotus' account: 4.157), and it is there that Apollo looks down, the nymph Cyrene beside him, as they dance in the chorus for his Carneia. The claim made for it – that it was 'more godly' than any other seen by Apollo – is, taken literally, a remarkable one: Apollo had many famous choruses, at Delos, at Delphi, and elsewhere. As

Callimachus goes on to explain, this is the beginning of a tradition of Apollo cult which the Battiads maintain through the subsequent centuries.

The Battiads are named rather than the citizens of Cyrene in general, and probably the Apollo cult was associated with the royal family in particular; Callimachus in this hymn is concerned with praise of 'my king' (lines 86–7) as well as of Apollo and of the city of Cyrene, and elsewhere identifies himself as a descendant of Battus, i.e. a member of the city's aristocratic elite (e.g. *Epigram* 35 Pfeiffer = 30 Gow and Page, quoted in the introduction).[3]

In the third century BC, this tradition of using myth-historical stories to link cities to other places in the Greek world through space and time is revived with a special intensity, as a way of handling the relationship between a newly expanded world and the Hellenic past (not by chance is the only surviving Hellenistic epic a story of wandering and places, including scenes in North Africa, i.e. the *Argonautica* by Apollonius of Rhodes). At the same time, literature includes praise for kings (and queens), for which models were again available in the literature of the archaic and classical periods composed in honour of tyrants (the long-established hereditary monarchy in Cyrene of Pindar's time was anomalous: usually monarchies in archaic and classical Greece were shorter-lived). In the case of Cyrene, given its location in North Africa, Callimachus' early readers would have found it easy to see its colonization as an analogue for the later foundation of Alexandria by the Macedonian Alexander, from a family which claimed Argive descent. We are concerned with two North African Greek cities, both of which wish to assert their links across space and time with the older Greek world to the north, and at this point both ruled as monarchies, but Cyrene, being much older, can serve to some degree as a model for Alexandria, with the songs and stories in Pindar and Herodotus already there as examples of the use of myth and history for this purpose.[4]

The *Hymn to Delos* and the 'nautilus' epigram: cult and dedication

The *Hymn to Delos* treats both geography and kingship in related and spectacular ways. We have already seen (in the previous chapter) the way in which this song features an extensive tour of the Greek mainland and islands, all miraculously mobile and able to move away from Asterie (i.e. Delos, whose mobility is paradoxically no longer remarkable within her own world). In the course of Asterie's travels, her unborn child, Apollo, prophesies from her womb to tell her not to give birth on the island of Cos (lines 162–95):

> But this word from her son held her back: 'Do not, mother,
> do not bear me there. I neither blame nor resent
> the island (it is graceful and rich in grazing if any is),
> but to it the Fates owe another god, 165
> most exalted blood of the Saviours! Beneath his diadem
> will come, not unwilling to be ruled by a Macedonian,
> the twin mainland and the islands of the sea,
> to the ends of the earth, and whence the swift horses
> carry the sun. He will know the ways of his father. 170
> And at some time a common struggle will come to us,
> in the future, when, bringing the barbaric knife against
> the Hellenes and rousing Celtic Ares,
> late-born Titans from the furthest West
> will rush, like snowflakes, as many 175
> as the stars, when they graze in greatest number in the sky
>
> [*here two lines are almost entirely missing*]
>
> and the plain of Crisa and Hephaestus' ravines
> are hard-pressed on all sides, and they see the rich smoke
> of a neighbour on fire, and no longer only hear about it, 180
> but now they will see by the temple the gleam of enemy
> phalanxes, and now beside my tripods they will see

swords and shameless shield-belts and the despised
shields which will mark out a wicked path for that mindless tribe,
the Galatians. Some of them will be my prize, some by the Nile,   185
having seen their bearers breathe their last in the fire,
will lie as the rich spoils of a hard-working king.
Ptolemy yet to be, these are Phoebus' prophecies for you!
For all your days you will greatly praise the one who prophesied
from the womb. But you, mother, consider this: 190
there is a slender island clearly visible in the water,
wandering through the seas. Her feet are not on the ground,
but she swims with the current like asphodel,
wherever the south wind, the east wind, wherever the sea carries her.
Give birth to me there: she will willingly receive you '   195

This is the most extensive passage of royal panegyric in extant Callimachus. The poet ties Ptolemaic rule from Egypt into the story of Delos and the birth of Apollo, both in time and in space. Before Apollo's birth the birth of Ptolemy, himself a god (line 165), is already prophesied, and he is associated with Macedonia in the north (the birthplace of his father) and Cos in the Aegean (his own birthplace) as well as with Egypt in the south, at the same time as his rule is predicted to extend across the known world (lines 166–70: the 'twin mainland' is a translation of an Egyptian expression used to refer to Egypt, upper and lower, but here adapted to suggest also 'Europe and Asia').[5] Ptolemy is a world ruler, but his history is tied into central aspects of Greek mythical history and geography. This Hellenic identity is emphasized even more where Apollo brings in his most important cult site *other* than Delos, i.e. Delphi, and the defeat there of the Celtic Gauls (i.e. Galatians; the invasion was in 279–278 BC). This is presented with the barbarian/Hellene dichotomy familiar from Persian Wars literature, and with Ptolemy as champion of the Hellenes. The 'Homeric' quality of the martial theme is emphasized by the similes (lines 175–6). Ptolemy is raised almost to the level of Apollo himself, and Alexandria to the south is a counterpart of Delphi to the north: Apollo explains that, of the spoils taken from the Gauls, some will be dedicated at Delphi, but some 'by the Nile' (line 185). Ptolemy is praised as a world-ruler (effectively an analogue for Alexander) and as a true heir to Ptolemy I his father (lines 166, 170): the latter is important since he was in fact the *younger* son of Ptolemy I, and thus not so obviously the heir as he might wish. While his rule is and will be world-wide, he remains a Hellene and a mighty defender of Hellas against the barbarian.

In an age of kings this must be taken seriously as panegyric, and it clearly speaks to the concerns of Ptolemy II and must have pleased him. Yet of course Cos is *not* Apollo's choice; his choice is the tiny island of Delos. In contrast with the smoke, the large scale and the violence of the prophecy concerning Ptolemy and his Homerizing victory, the island is 'slender' and 'clearly visible'. The latter (the Greek word is διειδομένη, *dieidomenē*) suggests a pun on the island's name: δῆλος (*delos*), as well as being the proper name for the island, is also an adjective, also meaning 'visible, clearly discernible' (contrasting with the smoke at Delphi). The adjective 'slender' (ἀραιή, *araiē*) suggests a metapoetic reading of the qualities of the island: we may remember that a different adjective with the same sense (λεπταλέην, *leptaleēn*) is used of the slim, lightweight qualities of Callimachus' preferred aesthetic as advocated by Apollo in the prologue to the *Aetia* (fr. 1.24).[6] With a view to the poetics expressed in the hymn, therefore, Bing reads the prophecy about Ptolemy as 'foil'.[7] The world of warfare, noise and smoke, and of martial poetry, is rejected and replaced by the 'slender' song of Callimachus, and the 'slender' island that represents it in this poem. Callimachus, in the world of the Ptolemies, can have his cake and eat it too: he includes extravagant praise of the king, but can still reject the noisy aesthetic of such celebration of martial great deeds in favour of the small and fine and transparent poetry symbolized by the island itself.[8]

The mobile island Asterie has a strange counterpart in a poem whose own scale is smaller, more slender than the *Hymn to Delos* (*Epigram* 5 Pfeiffer = 14 Gow and Page):

> I am a conch of old, but now you have me,
> Cypris of Zephyrion, as the first dedication of Selenaië,
> a nautilus who used to sail the seas, if the winds blew,
> holding out a sail from my own halyards,
> but if Galenaië, shining goddess of calm, was present, rowing energetically
> with my feet (see how my name fits my work!),
> until I was cast on the beach at Ioulis, so that I might become,
> Arsinoë, your much admired plaything.
> And no longer (I am a sailor no more) would the egg
> of the sea-moistened halcyon be hatched in my chambers as before.
> But show favour to the daughter of Cleinias, for she knows
> how to do good, and comes from Aeolian Smyrna.

Arsinoë, the sister and queen of Ptolemy II, was worshipped as Aphrodite in a temple at Zephyrion, on the coast of Egypt (it is unclear whether this happened before or after her death in 270 BC). This element in the Ptolemies' self-presentation as both kings (and queens) and gods was supported by poets. Callimachus' contemporary Posidippus composed three epigrams commemorating the dedication of the temple by the admiral Callicrates.[9] Callimachus' response is a startling one, recording a dedication by a woman, Selenaië, to Arsinoë/Aphrodite. The dedication is of a sea-shell, from a creature called a nautilus: the Greek word suggests 'sailor', and this is why the creature, which speaks on its own behalf, says that its name suits its activity (line 6): like a sailor, it can either row or sail, according to the weather. Some of the information that Callimachus has about this creature seems to come from Aristotle, who calls the nautilus 'a kind of octopus, very strange in both nature and behaviour' and, like Callimachus, describes it using language whose usual reference would be to human sea-faring.[10] Callimachus rewrites a 'scientific' description as found in Aristotle as poetry, adding extra detail (we do not know whether he invented or found elsewhere the idea that it was in the nautilus' shell that the semi-mythical sea-bird the halcyon laid its eggs). Aphrodite was associated with the sea, and the shrine at Zephyrium was a coastal one, so a sea-shell is perhaps an appropriate dedication. We do not know who Selenaië of Smyrna was, but as commentators point out, the places seem to resonate with Arsinoë's influence and history across the Aegean world. Smyrna was re-founded by Antigonus and Lysimachus, king of Thrace and Arsinoë's first husband, while the port of Ioulis, a city state on the Cycladic island of Ceos, was named Arsinoë after her, probably by the Ptolemaic admiral Patroclus.[11] Strikingly, then, Arsinoë is more than just the king's sister and wife; the narrator assumes that she will be well-disposed towards Selenaië because of her history before her marriage to Ptolemy as well as because of the Ptolemaic connection with Ioulis.

The little epigram has strange similarities with the large *Hymn to Delos*. In both cases, two 'persons' move about the Mediterranean world (Asteria and Leto, Selenaië and the nautilus: weirdly, the seashell, although masculine in grammatical gender, was 'pregnant' like Leto, since the halcyon's eggs used to be incubated in its shell). In both cases, the poem describes a movement from this mobility to fixity, as Delos becomes fixed in place after Apollo's birth, and as the formerly mobile nautilus is now in place on dry land (beside the sea) at Zephyrium. In both cases, the 'fixing' is associated with a new cult site, on Delos and at Zephyrium (in the latter case the *establishment* of the cult of Arsinoë-Aphrodite is not explicitly described, but it was of course a new cult, established in Arsinoë's lifetime or at her death). In both cases the new status quo is associated with dedication, and the movement towards orderly fixity is associated with Ptolemaic rule: the dedication of the rigging from the Athenians' ship (line 315) in the hymn may even seem to correspond to the sail and halyards of the nautilus in the epigram, while the prophecy concerning Ptolemy, as we have seen, also looks forward to the defeat of the Galatians and the dedication of armour both at Delphi and in Egypt.

Callimachus in both poems is working with an ideological pattern that associates the Ptolemaic regime with stability and with religious cult (including cult *of* Ptolemaic rulers) and links it to other parts of the Greek world spatially. The epigram reads as something aesthetically concerned with what is fine and delicate, and exemplifies Callimachus' ability to make poetry of the prosaic world of natural science, but at the same time it contributes to the ideological presentation of Arsinoë and of the Ptolemaic monarchy.

Place and praise in the *Aetia*

The *Aetia*, with its anthology-like structure, offers great opportunities to explore the geography of the new and old Greek worlds, with juxtapositions and clusters of stories relating to different places, as well as treatment of the Ptolemaic royal family. The reader is constantly reminded that stories from all around the Greek world are being told *from North Africa* (whether Egypt or Cyrene). Callimachus does not present himself as moving around in search of stories in the manner of Herodotus. In the first part this is achieved through having Muses answer his questions; probably at the start of the second book he also asks questions of a mortal interlocutor, a visitor from the island of Icus who is participating at a symposion in the house of an Athenian resident in Alexandria. The second half lacks this kind of narrative framing, but also marks out the narrator-poet's location in Africa. The third book began with an elegy commemorating the victory of Berenice II, queen of Cyrene by birth and of Egypt by marriage to Ptolemy III 'Euergetes', in the Nemean Games, and the narrator locates the performance in Egypt, while the whole collection ended with an account of the catasterism of a lock of hair dedicated by the same Berenice at the temple of Arsinoë/Aphrodite at Zephyrium, which we have already encountered above, and seems likely to have mentioned the Cyrenean heritage she shared with Callimachus himself.[12] So as the stories of the *Aetia* range around the Greek world they are constantly tied back into the world of Callimachus and his readers in Cyrene and Egypt.

Stories set elsewhere may also relate back to North Africa in different ways. We have already seen (above, pp. 21–4) the end of *Acontius and Cydippe*, from the third book (lines 50–77):

> From that marriage a great name would come about,   50
> for still your clan, the Acontiadae,
> inhabits Ioulis, rich in number and honours,
> Cean, and we heard of this your desire
> from ancient Xenomedes, who, once upon a time,
> set down the whole island in a mythological memoir,   55
> beginning with how it was inhabited by Corycian nymphs
> chased from Mount Parnassus by a great lion,
> (for this reason they call it Hydroussa), and how Cyrene's
> [...] lived in Caryae,
> and how people settled there from whom Zeus   60
> Alalaxios receives sacrifices accompanied by the cry of trumpets,
> Carians together with Leleges, and how it was given its changed name
> by Phoebus' and Melia's son Ceos.
> He put insolence and death by lightning, he put the sorcerer
> Telchines, and he put in his tablets the old man Demonax who,   65
> in his madness, cared nothing for the blessed gods,
> and he put the old woman Macelo, mother of Dexithea:
> only these two, when the gods destroyed the island for wicked
> insolence, did they leave unscathed.
> And he told how, of the four cities, Megacles built   70
> Carthaea, and Eupylus son of Chryso, half a goddess,
> built the citadel of Ioulis with its many springs, while Acaeus
> built Poeessa, shrine of the Graces with beautiful hair,

> and Aphrastus the town of Coresius, and he spoke, Cean,
> of your bitter love mixed with the story of these, 75
> that old man devoted to truth, from which the boy's
> story ran to our Calliope.

The book of Xenomedes of Ceos was a very 'local' piece of mythical history, concerned with the faithful reporting of the traditions of one island, which (as discussed previously) offer plenty of possible *aetia*. But from his work (and from his island) the story of Acontius has 'run' to Callimachus' Muse Calliope. In this re-imagining of literary inspiration in an age of books inspiration has moved through space and time from Xenomedes to Calliope and thus to Callimachus and the movement mirrors the movement of texts, in the form of books, from all over the Greek world to Alexandria and to the library. Callimachus' poem, as the library itself, symbolizes the transformation of Alexandria from periphery to centre, as Hellenic culture in the form of texts and stories and books moves southwards from the older Greek world to the new city.

Earlier in the same poem, Apollo at Delphi explains to Cydippe's father that Acontius is a lover of distinguished family, so that it will be no shame for him to marry his daughter to him (fr. 75.32–7):

> You, the bride's father, are descended from Codrus; he the Cean
> son-in-law, from the priests of Zeus Aristaeus
> the Icmian, whose concern is, on the crags of the mountain,
> to assuage harsh Maera as she rises, 35
> and to ask from Zeus for the wind by which numerous
> quails are dashed into nets of linen.

'Zeus Aristaeus' on Ceos is attested on coins from the islands' communities, and seems to be a conflation of a hero with a god that can be found in other examples elsewhere in Greek religion; on Ceos he is called 'Icmian' also in Apollonius of Rhodes and the later poet Nonnus.[13] Apollo, the speaker, seems to share the poet-narrator's interests in curious details of ritual (as well as in birds!): he describes the peculiar custom by which the Cean priests of Aristaeus pray for Maera, a name for the dog-star of the hottest days of summer, to be gentle (i.e. for the heat of summer not to be too intense) and for the coming of the cooling Etesian winds which are accompanied by migrating quails, caught on Ceos with the use of nets.[14] Just as Callimachus does himself in other parts of the same elegy, Apollo also hints at a possible *aetion*: how did the Ceans come to worship in this way? The answer is not provided by Callimachus here, but his contemporary Apollonius of Rhodes (*Argonautica* 2.498–527) tells how Aristaeus, the son of Apollo and Cyrene, having been born and brought up in Libya and then moved to Thessaly, was sent by Apollo to Ceos to save the inhabitants from a heatwave, which he accomplished by establishing a sanctuary of Icmian Zeus and sacrificing to the dog-star and to Zeus, who responded by sending cooling 'etesian' winds. In *Acontius and Cydippe*, in other words, north to south is not the only direction of cultural movement; Ceos is the source of the story of Acontius and of Xenomedes' book, but also the destination of a cultic foundation which, while it arrives in Ceos from the north, has its earlier roots in Libya and was established by the son of Cyrene herself. There is more than one way in which mythical material from peninsular Greece and the Aegean can be tied back to Callimachus' own North African world.

By this reading, the poem fits well into a Ptolemaic cultural programme in which Callimachus' own Cyrene also has a special place. The same elegy also contains this strange passage (fr.75.1–7; see pp. 24–6 above):

> ... and already the maiden had slept with a youth,
> since there was a custom ordering the bride to spend the night
>   before the wedding
> with a male child, both of whose parents were living.
> For, they say, once Hera – dog, dog, hold back, shameless

> spirit! You will sing even what religion forbids! 5
> It is fortunate that you have seen nothing of the rites of the
>   dread goddess,
> or you would have spewed out their story too.

Another *aetion* is side-stepped: *why* does a bride on Naxos spend her last night before the wedding with a boy whose parents are both alive? The poet-narrator starts to answer: something to do with Hera ... but suddenly interrupts himself and chastises himself for having been about to tell a story that religion should forbid him from telling. What was the story? An ancient commentator believed that the untold story related to the pre-marital sexual relationship between the siblings Zeus and Hera, and while this seems unlikely as a correct explanation for the Naxian ritual it is probably correct that this is what Callimachus wants his reader to think of.[15] The lines in the *Iliad* which refer to this (14.292 and following) were already cited in Plato as an example of a morally unsuitable theme in poetry (Plato *Republic* 3.390b–c), and quite possibly Callimachus means us to think of this as well. In the world of Callimachus, however, this is a strikingly odd thing to do, because the sibling marriage of Zeus and Hera could be seen as a model for the marriage of Ptolemy II with his sister Arsinoë.[16] Why, then, would Callimachus reject this story as so shocking?

It seems that in line 4 Callimachus is alluding to a poem by an older contemporary, Sotades, which has not survived but of which a fragment runs 'They say that once Hera, with Zeus who delights in thunder.'[17] This line probably opened the poem of Sotades which later contained his most famous and shocking line (Sotades fr. 1):

> it's an unholy hole he's shoving his prick in[18]

This was anciently interpreted as an insulting reference to Ptolemy's incestuous marriage.[19] This helps us to make more sense of Callimachus' reluctance to tell of the incest of Zeus and Hera (scarcely as much of a secret as he makes it sound, since it *was* described by

Homer): he rejects the insulting treatment by Sotades rather than the theme of the royal marriage as such. Except, of course, that by rejecting it – by making a song and dance of rejecting it – he surely calls attention to what is left unsaid and reminds his reader of Sotades' insult, which one might have imagined that Ptolemy would prefer forgotten.

Callimachus' treatment of this, his theatrical rejection of the story about Hera, testifies to a remarkably relaxed courtly atmosphere. While royal incest made sense in Egyptian terms it was shocking from a Greek perspective, yet Callimachus seems to bring up Sotades' shocking poem in a way which seems jocular and flippant, even if it also engages with Platonic discourse about propriety and poetry and with the praise motif of Zeus and Hera as analogues for the Ptolemaic marriage.[20] As Cameron suggests (talking about the *Lock of Berenice*, discussed below), 'it is ... surprising to find a court poet making any kind of joke about so delicate a topic as a king's incest'.[21] The Ptolemies were praised in Callimachus' poems, which can be seen to align themselves with the regime's cultural programme in numerous ways, as they also attest to Callimachus' identification with his own city of Cyrene and its elite class, but that praise seems to have been given in an atmosphere where careful sycophancy was not required.[22]

Praise of Ptolemaic *queens* was especially important in Callimachus' work, and the second half of the *Aetia* both opened and closed with poems in praise of the queen who followed Arsinoë, i.e. Berenice II, the wife of Ptolemy III 'Euergetes' (she married Ptolemy in 246, shortly before he ascended the throne). The third of the four books started with an elegiac epinician, i.e. a poem for a victory in an athletic competition, commemorating the victory of Berenice's chariot team in the Nemean Games. The poem is fragmentary, but the beginning survives (fr. 54 Harder, lines 1–10):[23]

> To Zeus and to Nemea I owe a pleasant gift,
> bride, sacred blood of the sibling gods,

our victory song [...] for your horses.
Just now, from cow-born Danaus' land,
to the island of Helen and the seer of Pallene,   5
the herdsman of seals, there came a golden word:
that by the tomb of Eupetes' son Opheltes
they ran, and did not warm the shoulders of charioteers in front
with their breath, but while they rushed
like the wind nobody saw their trace in the dust.   10

Praise for the victory is presented in a way which draws attention to Berenice's royal marriage, as she is called 'bride' and the word translated as 'gift' means 'dowry' in earlier Greek. She is referred to as 'sacred blood of the sibling gods' as if she were the daughter of Ptolemy II and Arsinoë: in fact her parents were Magas of Cyrene and Apama. This is a striking example of how the dynastic line of the Ptolemies was presented in Egypt: despite the shocking quality of full-sibling incest within a Greek value-system, the Ptolemies' commitment to the Pharaonic symbolism of pure-blood royal incest meant that they presented Ptolemy III and his wife as if they were brother and sister, and Callimachus plays along.[24] The presentation of the poem as a debt is Pindaric, and throughout Callimachus is looking back at early classical song as seen in lyric epinicians by Pindar and Bacchylides. The start of a Pindaric epinician frequently thematised movement in space and identified the victor's home-town, which usually seems to be the location of the first performance. Here the news itself has been transmitted to the poet (Callimachus was not at Nemea, and presents himself as turning others' reports to poetry).

The way in which he does so contributes to the broader project of tying North African places into the geography and mythical history of 'old' Greece. We have seen above (in the treatment of Cyrene) that Pindar does this too, and that the roots of this kind of mythical thinking are much older than Callimachus: for example, Pindar knew a story that the spring of Ortygia at Syracuse was connected under the sea with the river Alpheus, which flows through Olympia (*Nemean* 1.1–2; this must go back at least to the sixth century BC, since it was also mentioned by Ibycus: fr. 323). The story's origins lie in two closely connected desires of the Greeks of Syracuse: to stress their colony's connection with the world of peninsular Greece and the Aegean, and to emphasize their remarkable record of success at the prestigious crown games.[25] When Callimachus came to do something similar for Alexandria, the tradition had resources available to help him. As I have mentioned, in the archaic period the Greeks told of how Io had travelled to Egypt, from where her descendant Danaus made the return journey to Argos. When Callimachus refers to 'cow-born Danaus' land' in line 4, it is thus initially unclear whether he is referring to Egypt: only as we read on do we realize that the information is moving from Nemea (near Argos: 'Danaus' land' means 'Argos and its environs') to Egypt, and the initially confusing way in which the allusion is made emphasizes how intertwined Egypt and Argos are in myth. When he comes to the Egyptian end of the journey, Callimachus reaches for other places where Egypt occurs in myth: the island of Helen is by the harbour of Alexandria, and its name recalls the tradition, most clearly visible in Herodotus and Euripides but with roots as old as the lyric poet Stesichorus, that Helen went not to Troy but to Egypt, where there was local cult for her.[26] The seer of Pallene is the seal-herd Proteus, first seen at Pharos (site of the harbour of Alexandria) on the coast of Egypt in the *Odyssey*, where he prophesies to Menelaus on his way back from Troy.[27] This emphasis on mythical 'placing' of Egypt must have continued in another fragment, which probably belongs early in the poem. Fr. 54a Harder is too badly preserved to translate, but does give a number of suggestive proper names: Inachidae, the descendants of Inachus (Io's father); Amymone, one of Danaus' daughters; Aegyptus; Nile; Proteus. Clearly this part of the poem developed the mythological and genealogical ties between Egypt and Greece at greater length.

As in most of Pindar's and Bacchylides' lyric epinicians, so in Callimachus' elegiac one, it seems that the main part of the poem was taken up with a mythical narrative, and in Callimachus this was the story of Heracles' fight with the Nemean Lion: an appropriate myth for a celebration of a Nemean victory, especially since the elegy seems to have included an *aetion* for the use of a wreath of celery as the prize for the games (fr. 60c Harder = 54 Pfeiffer: this commentary on Vergil seems to draw on Callimachus' poem). Furthermore, the Ptolemies' dynastic claims involved Ptolemy I's descent from the Macedonian king Amyntas, which meant that they shared in the Macedonian royal family's claim that they were ultimately descended from Heracles, via Temenus of Argos (see already Herodotus 8.137, Thucydides 2.99). So both the stress on Argive relations with Egypt and the choice of Heracles' task as myth suit the Ptolemies' self-presentation and cultural politics.

All of this sounds very grand: a poem that celebrates the long royal lineage of an imperial monarchy with a tale of the slaying of a lion by the greatest of all the heroes of Greek myth. And yet the 'flavour' of this poem was very different from what this description might lead one to expect. On his way through the district of Nemea, Heracles comes upon the house of Molorcus. In this part of fragment 54b Harder (177 Pfeiffer), Molorcus explains to Heracles that the presence of the lion has prevented him from gathering fuel and his livestock from roaming, so that the hospitality he can provide is limited (lines 23–9):

> 'so that once again I may [receive] you with food for my fire,
> not in this state of miserable lack of wood
> as now – for the coppice is ignorant of the sickle
> while the bounding month of Nemea [...] (?),
> and the nanny-goat, longing to nibble the gorse,
> bleats, shut inside the gates [...]
> [...] the ill-tempered billy-goat [...]'

We can see here features we have seen elsewhere: the imaginative recreation of the world of animals (not talking this time), and an interest in the small and homely. This scene of frugal hospitality offered to a great hero seems very close to the *Hecale*.[28] Our longest fragment from this poem starts with a scene with a female serving a meal and then, after an epic-style expression of time, describes what Molorcus does while Heracles is fighting the lion (fr. 54c Harder = 177 Pfeiffer):

> [*one line almost completely missing*]
> [...] she lifted it with a wooden fork [...]
> [*one line almost completely missing*]
> [...] giving a portion to the son of [...].
> At the time when the evening star was about to loosen the
>   oxen's yoke,   5
> the shepherd's star, who comes at sunset
> [...] when the sun shines for the Ophionids
> [...] the older gods,
> [...] the door. And he, when he heard the sound,
> as when a lion roars at the ear of a timid hind,   10
> a lion cub, he waited a moment to listen and spoke quietly:
> 'Nuisances! Why have you come, our neighbours, to wear away
> our home, since you won't gain anything at all?
> Some god created you, to make your hosts wail!'
> With these words he threw aside his work, which [...],   15
> since he was preparing a hidden trick against the mice.
> Into twin traps he put destructive baits,
> taking darnel-flour mixed with hellebore
> [...] he concealed death
> [*one line almost completely missing*]   20
> [...] like falcons, falling [...]
> Often they licked the greasy oil from the lamp
> after drawing it out with their tails; when the lid was not placed
> on brines and bowls or when they pushed it off from another
> cupboard, and [...] the possessions of a poor man   25

[...] pressed under a hard stone
[...] they danced
on his forehead, and drove slumber from his eyelids.
But those ravening beasts did this deed in one short night,
the most shameless of all, which most made him rave with fury: 30
the wicked creatures gobbled up his clothes, his goatskin, his satchel!
For them he prepared twofold slaughter:
a trap with both a hammer and a spring that could leap a long way.

While Heracles slays the mighty lion, Molorcus deals with a different enemy: mice! The elaborate expression of time at lines 5–8 means 'in the evening': when the oxen stop working, and the sun sets into the world beneath, where the older gods live, descended from Ophion (in some versions of the myth of generations of gods Ophion corresponds to Uranus, two generations older than Zeus and his siblings).[29] This elaboration suggests epic, as does the use of simile at lines 10–11: Molorcus' battle with the mice is like an epic battle, while the lion of the simile reminds of the lion pursued by Heracles and encourages us to contrast the two situations ... but it is only a *little* lion (the word for 'cub' is delayed in the Greek and I have tried to reproduce this in translation), as the mice are little. The activities of the mice are described in engaging detail: not only do they eat up food and lamp-oil but also even Molorcus' clothes and his leather bag –so unafraid are they that they dance on his face and stop him from sleeping! We are gently reminded of the contrast and analogy between Molorcus' deed and Heracles': the mice are 'ravening beasts' (σίντης, *sintēs*, 'ravening' is a word used in Homer of lions and wolves), a term which would more naturally describe the lion; when the mice sneakily steal oil from the lamp by dipping their tails into it (lines 22–3) the word used for 'tail' (ἀλκαία, *alkaia*) is one most commonly used of *lions'* tails. Against these Molorcus contrives his traps, using both poison and mechanical devices (in 18 hellebore is a poison, and darnel poisonous to people, though perhaps not to mice;

at 32–3 probably one trap crushes the mouse and the other traps it where it will eat the poison).[30] This looks like a further *aetion*: the invention of the mouse-trap.

In this poem Callimachus aligns himself with the ideological programme of the Ptolemaic royal family in Egypt, their dynastic claims and their need to stress the connections and continuities through time and space between the world of Greek myth and contemporary Alexandria. He was able to do this while working within a system of thought with its roots much earlier, by redeploying mythological connections between Egypt and Greece which had already developed in the archaic period and used to help the Greeks to make sense of an expanding world as Greeks encountered Egypt as merchants or mercenaries rather than monarchs and settlers: stories of genealogical connections between Egypt and Argos, and of visits by personnel of the Trojan War. As a precedent for asserting such mythical connections in a traditional framework he had good models in earlier Greek poetry: earlier praise poets such as Pindar and Bacchylides did something similar for earlier generations of Greeks outside the 'old world' of Greece and the Aegean, especially in Sicily and (of particular significance for Callimachus) in Cyrene.

However, Callimachus works within this tradition in a distinctive and fresh style. He adapts his models for a new kind of dynasty, and in accordance with characteristic interests of his own poetry. In this case we see an interest in seeking out the humble and lowly character in a heroic tale that we saw in *Hecale*; and especially in the mice we see an interest in that which is small in scale and in animals that we have seen in *Hecale* and throughout Callimachus' work. By some readings of the prologue to the *Aetia*, it might feel as if Callimachus were rejecting 'kings and heroes' (fr. 1.3–5). But this would be a naively simplistic reading of the beginning of the poem, which blends together issues of subject matter, treatment and scale, rather than straightforwardly vetoing any subject matter. Handling the praise of a queen through telling of the most famous of heroes is something that Callimachus can take on in his own way, using the adaptation of material and models from the literature of the past to address the concerns of the present in a distinctive and individual manner.

Further reading

Acosta-Hughes and Stephens 2012, 148–203 is an excellent study of Callimachean places, and cf. Asper 2011 on Callimachean 'geopoetics', Barbantani 2011 on kingship, Prioux 2011 on queens, and Cameron 1995, 3–23 on Callimachus and the Ptolemaic court. Bing 2008 involves an extensive treatment of the *Hymn to Delos*.

Envoi: The End of the *Aetia*, and Callimachus in Rome

Close to the end of the *Aetia* is a startling reminder of a way in which Callimachus lived in a world which was soon going to change. Only a few words of the first line of this elegy survive; but the *diegesis* survives in full (fr. 107a Harder; vol. 1, 110 Pfeiffer):

> He says that, when the Peucetians were laying siege to the walls of Rome, one of the Romans, called Gaius, jumped on the man leading them and brought him down to the ground, and received a wound in his thigh. Afterwards, having become miserable about the fact that he was limping, he ceased from this depression when he was reproached for it by his mother.

We know little for sure about this: who is Gaius? His mother must have told him that he should take pride in his limp as a reminder of his courage. The story shows us that Callimachus knows not only of the Greek communities of southern Italy but also of the increasingly powerful city state which, after his death, would gradually come to dominate the whole Mediterranean. Callimachus, of course, did not know the future; but for us the world of Rome may play a part in how we understand his work, in ways which will become apparent.

We can reconstruct the sequence of stories at the end of book 4 in detail, because the *diegesis* from which I quoted above survives and gives us summaries. The story of Gaius was followed by the story of the origin of a stone anchor dedicated at Panormus in Cyzicus (on the coast of Asia Minor, on the Propontis): this had been left there by the Argonauts.[1] So a story of travel around the Mediterranean is picked up in the north-east of that world, and follows a story from the west; at this point the focus returns to Alexandria for the end of the work, an astonishing piece of 'occasional' praise poetry for Berenice, forming a pair with the epinician for Berenice which started book 3. This was the *Lock of Berenice*: it survives in fragments from papyri, and we have a remarkable extra witness in the form of Catullus 66, a Latin translation or adaptation of Callimachus' elegy. The occasion of the poem can be reconstructed in detail from various sources.[2] In 246 BC (shortly after the royal pair ascended to the throne), Ptolemy III went to war in Syria, and Berenice, his wife, vowed to dedicate a lock of her hair upon his safe return, probably at the temple of Arsinoë/Aphrodite at Zephyrium. When she made good on her vow in the following year, the court astronomer Conon recognized a new constellation and identified it as her lock, translated into the stars. This is 'court poetry': the poem celebrates a staged courtly event highlighting the quasi-divine status of the queen, and commemorating the loving relationship between the royal couple, which was an important aspect of Ptolemaic self-presentation.

As with the conch epigram (5 Pfeiffer = 14 Gow and Page, discussed above, pp. 99–101), Callimachus commemorates the event by having the dedication itself speak: the lock records its own dedication and catasterism in what can be described as a huge expansion of the form of a dedicatory epigram (Catullus' translation is 94 lines long; there is room for doubt whether this was exactly the length of Callimachus' elegy, but anyway it was far longer than any epigram). Here I have put together a translation of Greek fragments (presented in Roman type) supplemented from Catullus' Latin (*in italic type*), to show how the poem began:

> He who observed the whole firmament delineated and the movements
> *of the stars as they rise and set,*
> *how the fiery brightness of the rapid sun is darkened,*

> and how at fixed times stars depart,
> and how in secret love takes the Moon to the Latmian rocks
> and calls her away from her heavenly course:
> Conon saw me in the sky, Berenice's
> lock of hair, which she dedicated to all the gods.

As so often, Callimachus translates the stuff of prose into verse (the language of the first line is the technical language of astronomy), and (as discussed above, chapter 2) he rejoices in the capacity for the written word to create a voice. In a way which may be compared with the 'Tomb of Simonides' (fr. 64 Pfeiffer, discussed above, pp. 49–51), the object which might be expected to be the speaker is no longer in place (if the lock had an inscription in the temple, it is now separated from it), but in this case the lock has not been destroyed but has been taken to the stars, and can still speak in its own 'voice'.

The lock has a mind of its own, and rather resents its separation from Berenice's head even as it shares in some of the poet's knowledge and interests (lines 45–56 survive in Greek):

> ... the ox-piercer of your mother Arsinoë, and through the middle
> of Mount Athos went the destructive ships of the Medes.
> What are we locks of hair to do, when such mountains yield
> to iron? Let the race of the Chalybes be destroyed,
> who first brought it to light, this wicked shoot springing from the
>   earth,
> and first explained the work of hammers.
> My sister-locks were longing for me, newly cut off,
> and straightway the brother of Ethiopian Memnon
> rushed to me, a delicate breeze whirling his swift wings,
> the steed of Locrian Arsinoë with her violet girdle.
> He snatched me with his breath, and having carried me through
>   the moist air
> he set me in Cypris' lap ...

The lock is addressing Berenice herself, and explaining that it had no power to prevent itself from being cut: who can yield to iron? But it says this in a complex and obscure way! We do not know what Callimachus is referring to as the ox-piercer of Arsinoë (scholia explain 'ox-piercer' as meaning 'obelisk', so perhaps this is another mountain, in addition to Mount Athos in the following line), but it enables him to refer to the fiction that Berenice was the daughter of Arsinoë (as we have seen already in the epinician). The lock knows its Greek history, in any case, and can refer to Xerxes' canal through the promontory of Mount Athos as an example of the power of iron (cf., for example, Herodotus 7.22-4); in a very Callimachean fashion it can also tell of the 'origins' of iron-working (an embedded *aetion*), invented by the Chalybes, a people living to the north of the Black Sea. It knows genealogy: the wind, Zephyrus, is the brother of Memnon (who fought at Troy), because both are sons of Eos, the dawn (why Zephyrus is also called the 'horse of Locrian Arsinoë' is unclear). One of the words used for 'lock' is masculine (πλόκαμος, *plokamos*), but the word for hair used in line 51 (κόμη, *komē*) is feminine, and here the lock of hair does seem to be treated as female: it is abducted by a wind (a common mythological fate for young women), and it is missed by its fellow sister-locks (rather as a female is mourned by her companions when she leaves them for marriage: e.g. Sappho 94, 96).[3]

It feels as if an analogy is being developed between Berenice as bride and the lock, whose separation from her head is like the separation of a young woman from her companions. Even the lock's washing in the sea ('Cypris' lap') may echo the ritual bathing of bride and groom before marriage.[4] This imagery is continued later on. Lines 61-4 are preserved in Greek; the following lines are fragmentary or missing, but between what survives and Catullus' translation we can tell that they treated the catasterism in more detail, including a parallel between Ariadne's wreath (another constellation) and the new lock; lines 75-8 are then preserved complete.

counted among the many stars, but that I might shine also,
I, the beautiful lock of Berenice.
After washing me in the waters, Cypris brought me to the deathless ones
and placed me as a new star among the ancient ones.
[ten lines]
These things do not bring me delight as much as my grief
that I no longer touch that head
from which, when I was a girl, I drank many
oils, but did not enjoy the perfumes of a married woman.

The sense of this is that the lock of hair was oiled as part of Berenice's beauty regime as a young woman, but did not experience marriage and the use of perfume as an erotic practice of the married wife. It feels as if the analogy between the lock's removal and marriage is playing out differently here: now Berenice has got married, but the lock has not accompanied her in the movement from the world of girlhood to that of wife. Callimachus seems to be blurring Berenice's marriage to Ptolemy together with her dedication of the lock (they did not in fact occur together), and is ignoring the fact that Berenice's marriage to Ptolemy was her *second* marriage.[5]

The thematization of marriage seems stronger when we find an *aetion* close to the end of the elegy, in lines preserved only by Catullus, where the catasterism of the lock is the beginning of a custom by which brides pour libations from a jar to the deified Lock (Catullus 66.79–88: as we shall see, the status of these lines is controversial; I am still using italics for lines preserved only in Latin):

Now you, whom the torch has joined with longed-for light,
do not hand over your bodies to your soulmates
bearing your breasts as you throw aside your clothes
before the jar pours generous gifts to me –
your jar, wives who obey the law in a pure bed.
But she who has given herself to impure adultery –
let her wicked libations be drunk by the light dust, pointless:

I don't want gifts from unworthy women.
Instead, brides, always let concord,
always let everlasting love dwell in your homes.

The lock addresses brides everywhere and instructs them to pour libations to it – but this command is only for good wives, and adulterers' libations will be in vain. However, these lines are not only unrepresented in our Greek fragments: we can see from the papyrus preserving the very end of the poem that it *never* contained these lines, but did include a pair of final lines not represented in Catullus' poem. Why is this? The papyrus (*P. Oxy.* 2258) is not from a copy of the *Aetia* as a whole, but from a book (dating to the sixth or seventh century AD) which contained the *Hymns*, *Hecale*, parts of *Aetia* 3, the *Lock of Berenice* and Callimachus' epinician for Sosibius (fr. 384 Pfeiffer). Pfeiffer conjectured that, when he added the poem to his *Aetia*, Callimachus himself added the lines of which the text above is Catullus' translation, presumably because he wanted to add a more obvious *aetion* at the end. The text in the papyrus, by this argument, represents Callimachus' first version, as a free-standing piece of court poetry before it was added to the *Aetia*, which somehow managed to get transmitted independently to our late papyrus.[6]

An alternative school of thought, however, has paid attention to the place of the Latin translation in Catullus' work. The eroticization of the brides and the moral anxiety about adultery are both very characteristic of the pre-occupations of Catullus' work. Could he have inserted ten free-composed lines of his own poetry into his 'translation' of Callimachus?[7] In other places in Catullus 66 (where we can see the Greek original), the poet does not do anything as radical as this, but he is by no means a slavishly 'close' translator. On a smaller scale, his poem 70 is clearly modelled on an epigram of Callimachus (25 Pfeiffer = 11 Gow and Page), but takes its opening idea and structure in a quite different direction from Callimachus' poem. Here at the end of the *Lock of Berenice*, the ten lines absent from the papyrus might function as a kind of signature, a modification that (for the ideally 'knowing' and learned Roman reader, already familiar with Callimachus' elegy) marked out Catullus' own contribution and alteration of his model.[8]

Here I do not mean to come down on one side or another of this long-lasting debate, but rather to draw attention to a problem which occurs here at an extreme level: that understanding Callimachus' poem is tangled up with understanding what a Roman poet has done with it. Callimachus was an important figure in Roman poetry, and one whose importance is frequently marked fairly explicitly by poets interacting with his work, and this is true of traditionally very 'canonical' poets including Catullus, Propertius, Ovid and indeed Virgil. Thus, to take a famous example, the second half of Virgil's book of ten *Eclogues*, 'bucolic' poems whose most important model is Theocritus, begins like this (Virgil *Eclogue* 6.1–5):

> First in Syracusan verse my Thalia deigned to play;
> nor did my Muse blush to dwell in the woods.
> When I was about to sing of kings and battles, Cynthius plucked
> my ear and warned: 'A shepherd, Tityrus, should
> raise fat sheep, but speak a slender song!'

So: while his Muse, Thalia, started out with poetry associated with Syracuse (home town of Theocritus) and the woods (the countryside as the proper location of bucolic), Tityrus had then been going to raise his sights to grander themes, before Cynthius (i.e. Apollo) stopped him, in terms which closely echo Apollo's instruction to the young Callimachus as recalled in the prologue to the *Aetia* (fr. 1.23–4 Pfeiffer):

> [Remember, dear] singer: raise your sacrifice as fat as possible,
> but, good fellow, keep your Muse slim.

Virgil's bucolic alter ego Tityrus goes on to explain that for this reason he cannot sing the praises of the contemporary politician Varus and his military activities. This is a rather characteristic combination of motifs in Roman poetry of the late republic and early empire: reference to a passage of Callimachus that seems to express an aesthetic principle and a preference for the small and delicate is used to motivate the Roman poet's disinclination to participate in poetry on martial themes in praise of the powerful.[9]

As new papyrus fragments came to light during the twentieth century, increasing attention was paid to the significance of Callimachus for Roman poetry, whether in the fragments or in the *Hymns* and epigrams. To take a particularly striking example, still from Virgil, in a marvellously tiny article of 1984, Ruth Scodel and Richard Thomas pointed out that the poet mentions the river Euphrates three times: at *Georgics* 1.509 and 4.561, and at *Aeneid* 8.726. In each of these places, the river is named six lines from the end of the book. As the authors observe, this is not a coincidence: rather, it is a pattern of allusion to a Callimachean text discussed already (above, pp. 18–20). This is the end of Callimachus' *Hymn to Apollo* (lines 105–13):

> Envy spoke secretly in Apollo's ear:
> 'I do not admire the singer who sings not as much as the sea.'
> Apollo kicked Envy and spoke as follows:
> 'The stream of the Assyrian river is big, but it drags along
> many scourings from the land and much rubbish on its water.
> To Deo the Melissae do not bring water from everywhere,
> but the little stream that comes up pure and undefiled
> from a holy spring, the choicest essence.'
> Farewell, Lord! As for Blame, let him go where Envy dwells!

The 'Assyrian river' is the Euphrates; and it occurs six lines from the end of the hymn. Again we are concerned with a programmatic passage thematizing Callimachus' poetics and his preference for the small and delicate. Let us look at one of Virgil's alluding passages in a little more detail (*Georgic* 4.559–564, the end of the poem):

> These lines on the cultivation of fields and flocks I sang
> – of trees as well – while mighty Caesar thundered at the deep
> Euphrates in war, and as a victor among the willing peoples
> gave laws, and prepared his road to Olympus.
> At that time sweet Parthenope nourished me,
> Virgil, as I rejoiced in the studies of inglorious ease,
> I who played shepherds' songs, and as a bold youth
> sang of you, Tityrus, beneath the shade of a spreading beech.

Virgil not only activates the Euphrates motif, but combines it with the idea of Caesar (this is Octavian, i.e. the future Augustus) 'thundering': we think of Callimachus in the *Aetia* prologue declaring 'it is not for me to thunder, but for Zeus' (fr. 1.20 Pfeiffer). Yet this is a profoundly Roman poetic moment. The contrast of 'ease' (*otium*, 'leisure') with political and military activity, the implied reluctance to compose poetry celebrating the latter (but at this point the reader knows that Virgil will become the poet of the *Aeneid*), all of this comes at the end of a poem which functions in part as a hymn to the countryside of Italy (including Italy with Greek heritage: Parthenope is the nymph of Naples, once a Greek colony). All of this explicitly serves the poet's self-presentation: Virgil names himself, and identifies himself as the poet of the *Eclogues* (the last line quotes from the first line of the first *Eclogue*).

The influence of Callimachus on Roman poetry is of course much more important than a few tags from particularly programmatic, metapoetic passages such as the examples just discussed. However, reading Callimachus through a Roman lens can lead to misunderstanding and a diminution of his poetic achievement and interest. Many readers (myself included) first came to Callimachus through the study of Roman poetry. This can result, first of all, in a view of Callimachus which stresses above all his poetics, and his poetics as they were filleted for use in different historical circumstances by Roman poets. Thus, for example, we have seen that the contrast between epic and elegy does not seem particularly relevant or helpful for the understanding of the poetic pronouncements of the prologue to the *Aetia*; yet it is very hard for many readers to let go of the idea that rejection of epic is what is at stake here, and a large part of the reason for this must be the strength of the contrast between epic and elegy in Roman elegy and the tensions produced in Roman poetry more than two centuries after Callimachus by the demand for epic poetry celebrating political and military achievements (most conspicuously by Octavian/Augustus). In Roman poetry, profession of 'Callimachean' poetics tends to be used in connection with this generic contrast and with contrast with or rejection of heroic epic, and for readers who have characteristically encountered canonical Roman poetry *before* Callimachus it may constitute an anachronistic but comfortably familiar 'frame' in which to situate Callimachus' work.

Secondly, thinking of Callimachus as a precursor to the Roman poets can lead to a reading which, while it neglects richer historicism, over-emphasizes a schematic form of literary history. We should not read Callimachus for his anticipations of Virgil (or Catullus, or Ovid), in a way which emphasizes his 'lateness' in relation to more canonical Greek poetry of the archaic and classical periods. Callimachus is too complex and too interesting to be seen as an intermediate stepping-stone between Euripides and Catullus. This is one of the reasons why, in this book, I have tried to emphasize strong elements of continuity between the classical and Hellenistic periods, even while acknowledging the significance of political and cultural changes, and to contextualize Callimachus in his own time.

The Roman poets of course had reasons to go to Callimachus for the aesthetic and metapoetic pronouncements which we have seen (and this is not the *only* thing they do with Callimachus); and Callimachus was extremely influential on poets such as Virgil, Propertius, Ovid, and others – and as such on the whole of the subsequent history of European literature.[10] In the case of the *Lock of*

Berenice, the evidence from which we are working means that trying to make sense of Callimachus' reception by Catullus is inseparable from the interpretation of his poem. In the light of the 'second renaissance' of papyrological discovery, however, scholarship gets better and better at seeing Callimachus' work as an object of fascination in its own right and set in its own Hellenistic world, while modern readers have more help to read Callimachus for enjoyment of his imagination, his wit, his capacity for striking juxtapositions and his ability to bring plural voices to light.

Further reading

There are useful discussions in Acosta-Hughes and Stephens 2012, 204–74, Hunter 2006 and Barchiesi 2011. For Virgil (and not only Virgil) see especially the papers gathered in Thomas 1999.

Notes

Introduction

1. Translations are my own unless otherwise indicated.
2. The new Posidippus papyrus may give an indication of what a single-author epigram collection would have looked like: see Austin and Bastianini 2002, nos. 1–112.

Chapter 1

1. On writing and books in Hellenistic poetry, see especially the first part of Bing 2008, including 29–38 on 'talking books'.
2. On Callimachus and the *Lyde*, see, for example, Krevans 1993.
3. *AP* indicates a number in the 'Palatine Anthology', the medieval manuscript which is our main source of ancient epigrams.
4. Williams 1978 on lines 105–13, with appendix; but contrast, for example, Cameron 1995, 403–9.
5. For this and more comparison with Pindar, see Morrison 2007, 135–7.
6. See Stephens 2015, 98.
7. On acrostics see, for example, Danielewicz 2005.
8. Fantuzzi and Hunter 2004, 63–6.
9. Harder 2012, ii.550–1.
10. For fuller discussion with bibliography, see Harder 2012, ii.32–44.
11. Harder 2012, i.121–3.
12. On Aesop and the fable in Callimachus, see Acosta-Hughes and Scodel 2004, treating this passage on pp. 5–8.
13. I translate the text in West 2005; for the connection with Callimachus, see, for example, Rawles 2006, 7.
14. For these lines and for Plato in the *Aetia* prologue, see Hunter 1989, Acosta-Hughes and Stephens 2012, 31–47.

15 At Fantuzzi and Hunter 2004, 75, we find the attractive suggestion that the narrator's old age, weighing him down, might correspond metaphorically to knowledge of the past and consciousness of tradition from which the poet seeks to escape and to become the 'light, winged' poet of inspiration.
16 Hollis 1997; his edition was Hollis 2009 (1st ed. 1990).
17 On 'scholarship' and the construction of an authorial persona in Callimachus, see, for example, Morrison 2007, 103–5.

Chapter 2

1 Cf., for example, Acosta-Hughes and Stephens 2002.
2 Acosta-Hughes 2014 includes a useful treatment of quasi-'Hellenistic' features in earlier poetry.
3 Cameron 1995, 76–95 argues for the *symposium* (drinking party) as the main performance context for epigrams; he was arguing against earlier accounts by which epigrams were mainly composed as 'book-poetry'.
4 Gow and Page 1965, ii.178.
5 For a more extensive reading of this poem with attention to the themes on which I focus here, see Rawles 2018b, with further bibliography.
6 Cf. Acosta-Hughes and Stephens 2012, 200–1.
7 Acosta-Hughes 2002, 191.
8 This is not a complete list of the possible intersections with other Callimachean poems: see Acosta-Hughes 2002, 191–2 (but remember that many of the poems are not securely dated).

Chapter 3

1 Hunter 1992.
2 For a study of the importance of the Egyptian context for Ptolemaic poetry, including Callimachus, see Stephens 2003.
3 Cf., for example, the title of Burn 1960.

4   The papers gathered in Hunter and Rutherford 2009 are interesting for thinking about the continuity of practice across a long time scale here. On later choruses, see, for example, D'Alessio 2016 (part of an ongoing project on this topic). Some of our earliest substantial musical texts are from cult songs at Delphi recorded in inscriptions of the Hellenistic period: see West 1992, 288–301.
5   Haslam 1993.
6   Haslam 1993, 119.
7   Haslam 1993, 125.
8   On Callimachus and worlds of performance, see especially Cameron 1995, chapter 2; on the *Hymns*, pp. 63–7.
9   On the identification of the king, see Stephens 2015, 18–19, with references.
10 Cf. Stephens 2015, 73.
11 Cameron 1995, 7–8.
12 Petrovic 2011.
13 Petrovic 2011, 271: I quote Petrovic's translation.
14 The inscriptions date from the fourth century BC onwards. See again Petrovic 2011, 266–73.
15 Petrovic 2011, 276–82.
16 Haslam 1993, 116 n. 9.
17 Cf. Stephens 2015, 49–50. The prominence of Aeschylus in the literary tradition of impressive hymns to Zeus may remind us of the contrast between Aeschylus and Euripides in Aristophanes' *Frogs*, alluded to by Callimachus in the prologue to the *Aetia* (cf. above, pp. 32–3). Callimachus, of course, rejects the noisy bombast of the Aeschylean sublime.
18 Haslam 1993, 116 dismisses such a 'serious' interpretation of the lines: for him, while Callimachus gestures at piety ('covers his ass'), this kind of rhetoric is ultimately 'a subterfuge' and inconsistent with serious praise.
19 On different kinds of motion in this hymn, see Bing 2008, 125–8.
20 An extra layer of ambiguity concerns the word translated here as 'oak': δρῦς, *drus*. In line 81, where the *drus* is the 'age-mate' of *Melie*, one might assume that it is not the *same* tree as the ash. But the word can be a general term 'tree' as well as referring specifically to the oak, in which case the question in 83, and the answer that follows, apply to *Melie* the ash-nymph

herself as much as to the oaks of Helicon. As more generally in this passage, the question is, 'How precisely should we read these correspondences?'

21 For a more extensive treatment of this passage, see Bing 2008, 40–4; more briefly, Stephens 2015, 194–5.
22 Cf., for example, Mineur 1984 ad loc., with references.
23 Cf. Plato *Phaedo* 58a-b. This is the only reference to Athens in Callimachus' poem: the island was detached from Athenian rule in 314 BC and during the third century was first controlled by the Antigonids before falling into the Ptolemaic sphere of influence in 286 BC (Stephens 2015, 159).
24 This emphasis on very 'human' maternal experience is then picked up in the treatment of the nymph Chariclo in the fifth hymn; both of the last pair of hymns, not treated here (but see Hunter 1992), include extensive focus on the suffering of parents.

Chapter 4

1 On the relationship between different narratives of the foundation of Cyrene, see Osborne 2009, 8–17. I use the term 'myth-historical' because such stories frequently blend elements which modern scholars would usually count as 'myth' (e.g. Oedipus and his descendants) with ones which might count as 'history' (Aristoteles/Battus was probably a historical person).
2 The story was told in the Hesiodic *Catalogue of Women* (frr. 124–7 Merkelbach and West 1967 = 72–6 in Most 2006).
3 Magas of Cyrene, by this reading the king referred to in lines 26–7, was not in reality a descendant of Battus, but he may well have adopted symbolic features of the Battiad monarchy, which had ended in the mid-fifth century; an inscription records that he served as priest of Apollo (*SEG* 18:743, *c.* 290–280 BC).
4 Compare Acosta-Hughes and Stephens 2012, 163–4.
5 Stephens 2015, 207.
6 Cf. Bing 2008, 119–20. At the time when Bing wrote this, it was believed that another effectively synonymous adjective, λεπτός, should be read at

fr. 1.11; but more recent scholarship has suggested otherwise. See Harder 2012, ii.41–3.
7   Bing 2008, 119, and more broadly his whole reading of this poem.
8   By my argument, Callimachus' contemporary Theocritus does something similar in his encomium for another king, Hieron II of Syracuse: Rawles 2018a, 265–8.
9   Posidippus epigrams 12 and 13 in Gow and Page 1965, known from a papyrus and from Athenaeus (116 and 119 in Austin and Bastianini 2002), and 39 in Austin and Bastianini 2002, from another papyrus discovered since Gow and Page's book.
10 Aristotle *Historia Animalium* 622b5: in particular, Aristotle also describes the shellfish as using a 'sail'. Cf. Gow and Page 1965, 169.
11 Cf. Gow and Page 1965, 171 (Smyrna); *New Pauly* sv. Patroclus [2] with *IG* XII,5: 1061 (Arsinoē as the port of Ioulis).
12 See Acosta-Hughes and Stephens 2012, 170–3 for a fuller account which I am drawing on here.
13 Harder 2012, ii.616. Ancient sources claim that Icmian means 'moist', because it is associated with the moist wind mentioned in 36.
14 There is an untranslatable suggestion of an etymology, by which the Etesian winds get their name from the verb αἰτέω (*aiteō*), translated as 'ask for'.
15 Cf. Harder 2012, ii.584–5. The ancient commentator is a scholiast on *Iliad* 14.294–6, where Zeus sees Hera and is filled with lust as he had been 'when they first mingled in love, frequenting their bed and keeping it secret from their own parents'.
16 Cameron 1995, 19–20.
17 Sotades fr. 16.
18 I borrow the translation from Cameron 1995, 18.
19 However, the tradition that he was executed for it must be false: Cameron 1995, 18–19.
20 Harder 2012, ii. 585 seems to me to underplay this aspect.
21 Cameron 1995, 22.
22 Compare Theocritus 14.60–4, where Ptolemy is praised not only for generosity and personal excellence in general, but also as 'cultured and a lover' (φιλόμουσος, ἐρωτικός).

23 Because papyri have come to light since Pfeiffer's edition, his numbering system does not work for this poem, so I am following Harder's 2012 edition instead. This fragment is made from fr. 383 Pfeiffer combined with *SH* 254.
24 This is also visible in inscriptions of the time: Harder 2012, ii.397.
25 On epinician poetry and the colonial milieu of the sixth and fifth centuries BC, see Hornblower 2004, 26–7, 103–28.
26 Stesichorus fr. 192 *PMG*, Herodotus 2.113–15, Euripides *Helen*.
27 Homer *Odyssey* 4.349–70.
28 Cameron 1995, 446–7; Ambuhl 2004.
29 Harder 2012, ii.443–4.
30 Harder 2012, ii.460–1.

Envoi

1 Cf. Apollonius of Rhodes *Argonautica* 1.948–60: both poems are concerned with the spread of Greeks through the Mediterranean world.
2 See Harder 2012, ii.796 for sources.
3 Gutzwiller 1992 is particularly strong on the connections between the *Lock of Berenice* and women's voices in poetry.
4 See Oakley and Sinos 1993, 15–16.
5 The entry for Berenice II by Ameling in the *New Pauly* gives a brief account of her adventurous life. Her first marriage was to Demetrius the Fair, but she had him murdered before marrying Ptolemy, thereby bringing Cyrene back under Ptolemaic rule.
6 Pfeiffer suggests this in the apparatus criticus of his edition: i.121.
7 Thus, for example, Putnam 1960, Cameron 1995, 105–6: for more bibliography on this question, see Harder 2012, ii.847.
8 For Catullan 'translation' in this poem see, for example, Clausen 1970.
9 For a comprehensive reading of this eclogue in relation to Callimachus' *Aetia*, see Clauss 2004.
10 See, for example, Thomas 1983 and 1993.

Bibliography

Acosta-Hughes, B. (2002) *Polyeideia: The Iambi of Callimachus and the Archaic Iambic Tradition*, Berkeley, CA.

Acosta-Hughes, B. (2014) 'The Prefigured Muse: Rethinking a Few Assumptions on Hellenistic Poetics', in J. J. Clauss and M. Cuypers, eds, *A Companion to Hellenistic Literature*, Malden, MA, 81–91.

Acosta-Hughes, B., L. Lehnus and S. Stephens, eds (2011) *Brill's Companion to Callimachus*, Leiden.

Acosta-Hughes, B. and R. Scodel (2004) 'Aesop poeta: Aesop and the Fable in Callimachus' *Iambi*', in M. A. Harder, R. F. Regtuit and G. C. Wakker, eds, *Callimachus 2 (Hellenistica Groningiana 7)*, Leuven, 1–21.

Acosta-Hughes, B. and S. Stephens (2002) 'Re-reading Callimachus' "*Aetia*" Fragment 1', *Classical Philology* 97, 238–55.

Acosta-Hughes, B. and S. Stephens (2012) *Callimachus in Context: From Plato to the Augustan Poets*, Cambridge.

Ambuhl, A. (2004) 'Entertaining Theseus and Heracles: The *Hecale* and the *Victoria Berenices* as a Diptych', in M. A. Harder, R. F. Regtuit and G. C. Wakker, eds, *Callimachus II (Hellenistica Groningiana 7)*, Leuven, 23–47.

Asper, M. (2011) 'Dimensions of Power: Callimachean Geopoetics and the Ptolemaic Empire', in B. Acosta-Hughes, L. Lehnus and S. Stephens, eds, *Brill's Companion to Callimachus*, Leiden, 155–77.

Austin, C. and G. Bastianini (2002) *Posidippi Pellaei quae supersunt omnia*, Milan.

Barbantani, S. (2011) 'Callimachus on Kings and Kingship', in B. Acosta-Hughes, L. Lehnus and S. Stephens, eds, *Brill's Companion to Callimachus*, Leiden, 178–200.

Barchiesi, A. (2011) 'Roman Callimachus', in B. Acosta-Hughes, L. Lehnus and S. Stephens, eds, *Brill's Companion to Callimachus*, Leiden, 509–33.

Bing, P. (2008 [1st ed. 1988]) *The Well-Read Muse: Present and Past in Callimachus and the Hellenistic Poets*, Ann Arbor, MI.

Blum, R. (1991) *Kallimachos: The Alexandrian Library and the Origins of Bibliography* (trans. H. F. Wellisch), Madison, WI.

Bulloch, A. (1984) 'The Future of a Hellenistic Illusion: Some Observations on Callimachus and Religion', *Museum Helveticum* 41, 209–30.

Burn, A. R. (1960) *The Lyric Age of Greece*, London.

Cameron, A. (1995) *Callimachus and His Critics*, Princeton, NJ.

Clausen, W. (1970) 'Catullus and Callimachus', *Harvard Studies in Classical Philology* 74, 85–94.

Clauss, J. J. (2004), 'Vergil's Sixth Eclogue: The *Aetia* in Rome', in M. A. Harder, R. F. Regtuit and G. C. Wakker, eds, *Callimachus II* (*Hellenistica Groningiana* 7), Leuven, 71–93.

Clauss, J. J. and M. Cuypers (2014) *A Companion to Hellenistic Literature*, Malden, MA.

D'Alessio, G. B. (2016) 'Didymaean Songs (on *SEG* 58.1301, 60.1150)', *MD* 76, 197–212.

Danielewicz, J. (2005) 'Further Hellenistic Acrostics: Aratus and Others', *Mnemosyne* 58, 321–34.

Fantuzzi, M. and R. Hunter (2004) *Tradition and Innovation in Hellenistic Poetry*, Cambridge.

Gow, A. S. F. and D. L. Page (1965) *The Greek Anthology: Hellenistic Epigrams*, Cambridge.

Gutzwiller, K. (1992) 'Callimachus' *Lock of Berenice*: Fantasy, Romance, and Propaganda', *American Journal of Philology* 113, 359–85.

Gutzwiller, K. (2007) *A Guide to Hellenistic Literature*, Malden, MA.

Harder, A., ed. (2012) *Callimachus. Aetia*, Oxford.

Haslam, M. (1993) 'Callimachus' *Hymns*', in M. A. Harder, R. F. Regtuit and G. C. Wakker, eds, *Callimachus* (*Hellenistica Groningiana* 1), Groningen, 111–25.

Hollis, A. S. (1997) 'A Fragmentary Addiction', in G. W. Most, ed., *Collecting Fragments / Fragmente Sammeln*, Göttingen, 111–23.

Hollis, A. S. (2009 [1st ed. 1990]) *Callimachus. Hecale*, Oxford.

Hornblower, S. (2004) *Thucydides and Pindar: Historical Narrative and the World of Epinikian Poetry*, Oxford.

Hunter, R. L. (1989) 'Winged Callimachus', *ZPE* 76, 1–2.

Hunter, R. L. (1992) 'Writing the God: Form and Meaning in Callimachus, Hymn to Athena', *MD* 29, 9–34.

Hunter, R. L. (2006) *The Shadow of Callimachus: Studies in the Reception of Hellenistic Poetry at Rome*, Cambridge.

Hunter, R. L. (2011) 'The Gods of Callimachus', in B. Acosta-Hughes, L. Lehnus and S. Stephens, eds, *Brill's Companion to Callimachus*, Leiden, 245–63.

Hunter, R. L. and I. Rutherford, eds (2009) *Wandering Poets in Ancient Greek Culture: Travel, Locality and Pan-Hellenism*, Cambridge.

Krevans, N. (1993) 'Fighting Against Antimachus: The *Lyde* and the *Aetia* Reconsidered', in M. A. Harder, R. F. Regtuit and G. C. Wakker, eds, *Callimachus* (*Hellenistica Gronigiana* 1), Groningen, 149–60.

Lloyd-Jones, H. and J. Rea (1969) 'Callimachus frr. 260–1 Pf. (*SH* 288–9)', *HSCPh* 72, 126–45; reprinted in *Greek Comedy, Hellenistic Literature, Greek Religion, and Miscellanea: The Academic Papers of Sir Hugh Lloyd-Jones*, Oxford, 1990, 131–52.

Lombardo, S. and D. Rayor (1988) *Callimachus: Hymns, Epigrams, Select Fragments*, Baltimore, MD.

Mair, A. W. and G. R. Mair (1955) *Callimachus: Hymns and Epigrams. Aratus* (*Loeb Classical Library* 129), Cambridge, MA.

Merkelbach, R. and M. L. West (1967) *Fragmenta Hesiodea*, Oxford.

Mineur, W. H. (1984) *Callimachus: Hymn to Delos*, Leiden.

Morrison, A. (2007) *The Narrator in Archaic Greek and Hellenistic Poetry*, Cambridge.

Most, G. W. (2006) *Hesiod* (2 vols) (*Loeb Classical Library*), Cambridge, MA.

Nisetich, F. (2001) *The Poems of Callimachus*, Oxford.

Oakley, J. H. and R. H. Sinos (1993) *The Wedding in Ancient Athens*, Madison, WI.

Osborne, R. (2009) *Greece in the Making, 1200–479 BC*, London.

Petrovic, I. (2011) 'Callimachus and Contemporary Religion: The *Hymn to Apollo*', in B. Acosta-Hughes, L. Lehnus and S. Stephens, eds, *Brill's Companion to Callimachus*, Leiden, 264–87.

Pfeiffer, R. (1949–53) *Callimachus* (2 vols), Oxford.

Pfeiffer, R. (1968) *A History of Classical Scholarship: From the Beginnings to the End of the Hellenistic Age*, Oxford.

Prioux, E. (2011) 'Callimachus' Queens', in B. Acosta-Hughes, L. Lehnus and S. Stephens, eds, *Brill's Companion to Callimachus*, Leiden, 201–24.

Putnam, M. C. J. (1960) 'Catullus 66.75–88', *Classical Philology* 55, 223–8.

Rawles, R. (2006) 'Notes on the interpretation of the "New Sappho"', *ZPE* 157, 1–7.

Rawles, R. (2018a) *Simonides the Poet: Intertextuality and Reception*, Cambridge.

Rawles, R. (2018b) 'Simonides on Tombs and the "Tomb of Simonides"', in N. Goldschmidt and B. Graziosi, eds, *Tombs of the Ancient Poets: Between Literary Reception and Material Culture*, Oxford, 51–68.

Reynolds, L. D. and N. G. Wilson (1991) *Scribes and Scholars: A Guide to the Transmission of Greek and Latin Literature*, Oxford.

Scodel, R. and R. F. Thomas (1984) 'Virgil and the Euphrates', *American Journal of Philology* 105, 339.

Stephens, S. (2003) *Seeing Double: Intercultural Poetics in Ptolemaic Alexandria*, Berkeley, CA.

Stephens, S. (2015) *Callimachus: The Hymns*, Oxford.

Thomas, R. F. (1983) 'Callimachus, the *Victoria Berenices*, and Roman Poetry', *Classical Quarterly* 33, 92–113.

Thomas, R. F. (1993) 'Callimachus Back in Rome', in M. A. Harder, R. F. Regtuit and G. C. Wakker, eds, *Callimachus* (*Hellenistica Gronigiana* 1), Groningen, 197–215.

Thomas, R. F. (1999) *Reading Virgil and His Texts: Studies in Intertextuality*, Ann Arbor, MI.

Trypanis, C. A., T. Gelzer and C. Whitman (1975) *Callimachus: Aetia, Iambi, Hecale and Other Fragments. Musaeus: Hero and Leander* (*Loeb Classical Library* 421), Cambridge, MA.

West, M. L. (1992) *Ancient Greek Music*, Oxford.

West, M. L. (2005) 'The New Sappho', *ZPE* 151, 1–9.

Williams, F. (1978) *Callimachus. Hymn to Apollo*, Oxford.

Index

Achilles 57
acrostics 19–20
Aeschylus 33, 78, 93
Aesop *see* fable
Alexander 'the Great' 2–3, 5
Alexandria 2–7, 95, 108, 112
animals 34–40, 99–100, 109–12,
    see also birds, cicadas
Antimachus 17–20
Aphrodite 66, 86, 99–100, 102,
    116
Apollo 18–20, 32–3, 56–7, 70–5,
    78–81, 85, 87, 91–2, 94–8,
    100, 103–4, 121
Apollonius of Rhodes 95, 104
Aratus 16–17, 20
Argo 92
Argos 93, 108, 113
Aristaeus 103–4
Aristophanes 8, 33
Aristotle 99–100
Arsinoë II 4–5, 47, 99–101, 105–6,
    117–18
Asteria *see* Delos
Athena 55, 61
Athens 52–7, 61, 86–7
Augustus *see* Octavian

Bacchylides 107, 112
Battus 1–2, 70, 91–2
Berenice II, 101–2, 106–7, 116–19
Bing, Peter 98
birds 32, 37, 55–7, 59–62, 85, 103–4
books and writing 15–18, 22–4,
    27–8, 33, 38–44, 45–51,
    103

Callimachus
  life 1–9
  poetic works 9–12

Aetia 4, 20–40, 49–51, 71,
    101–13, 115–22
Apotheosis of Arsinoë 4
Epigrams 1–2, 15–18, 47–9, 66,
    99–101, 116, 120
Hecale 41–3, 52–7, 61, 110,
    112
Hymns 18–20, 65–101, 122–3
Iambi 58–64, 67–8
prose works 6–7, 15–16
and Roman poetry 30, 115–25
Cameron, Alan, 106
Catullus 116–17, 119–21, 124–5
Cecrops 61
Ceos 22–3, 100, 103–4
Choniates, Michael 42–3
choruses 18–19, 64, 67, 70–2, 79–81,
    85–8, 94–5
cicadas 34–40
clothing 52–4
colonization 70, 91–5
Conon (of Samos, astronomer)
    116–17
Cos 84, 96–7
Crete 76, 86–7
criticism, literary *see* poetics and
    literary criticism
cult *see* ritual and cult
Cyclades 86
Cypris *see* Aphrodite
Cyrene 1–3, 18, 70–1, 74, 91–5,
    101–2, 104, 106, 113

Danaids 93
Danaus 93, 108
dedications 46–8, 86–7, 99–101,
    116–17
Deliades 85
Delos 20–1, 69, 79–88, 96–8, 100
Delphi 20–1, 79, 97–8

Demeter 18–19, 25
Demetrius Poliorcetes 66

Egypt 4–5, 66–7, 93, 97–102, 108, 113
elegy 30–2, 37, 123–4
Epaphus 93
epic 15–16, 30–1, 37, 52–4, 71–2, 95, 123–4
epigram and inscription 46–51, 116–17
epinician *see* praise, Pindar, Bacchylides
Euhemerus 68
Euphrates 19–20, 73, 122–3
Euripides 8, 33

fable 34, 58–64

Gauls 97–8

Haslam, Michael 68–9, 75, 89
Helen 108
Hera 24–5, 82, 84–5, 93, 104–6
Heracles 48, 92, 109–13
Herodotus 92, 95, 118
Hesiod 17, 77
Hesperus 86
Hipponax 58, 67–8
Hollis, A. S. 43
Homer 15–16, 26–8, 52–4, 57, 77–8, 97–8, 105–6
Homeric Hymns 71–2, 78–9
horniness, wine-induced 46

incest 4–5, 25, 67, 105–7
inscriptions 46–7
Io 93, 108

kings and queens, worshipped as gods 66–7, 99–101

Leto 81–2, 84, 87, 100
libraries 5–7, 15–16, 27, 38–41, 103

Libya *see* Cyrene
literary criticism *see* poetics and literary criticism

Macedonia 2–5, 95, 97, 109
Magas of Cyrene 3–4, 70–1, 107
marriage 118–20
medicine 24–5
metamorphosis 34–40
Mimnermus 30–3
Molorcus 109–12
mousetrap, invention of 110–12
Museum 5
myth 2, 23, 35–6, 40, 72, 79, 85–7, 92–3, 95, 108–13

Naxos 24–5, 105
Nemea 106–7
nymphs 83

Octavian 123–4
Odysseus 26–7
Ovid 121

paean 72
panegyric *see* praise
papyri 10–11, 28, 41–2, 120
Pelasgus 93
performance 8–9, 38–40, 64, 67–72, 85–9
Petrovic, Ivana 73
Pfeiffer, Rudolf 41, 120
Philetas 31–2
philology *see* scholarship
Pindar 8, 19, 34, 37, 72, 92–3, 95, 107–9, 112
Plato 36–40, 105–6
poetics and literary criticism 16–20, 28–40, 63, 72–5, 78–9, 98–9, 112–13
Posidippus 99
poverty *see* wealth and poverty
praise 3–4, 17–19, 61, 77–9, 85, 91, 95–102, 106–13, 116–20

Propertius 121
prophecy 56–7, 84
Proteus 108
Ptolemy I 'Soter' 3–4
Ptolemy II 'Philadelphus' 4–5, 77–8, 91, 96–9, 105–6
Ptolemy III 'Euergetes' 101, 107, 116

religion 5, 65–90
ritual and cult 21, 24–6, 64, 67–74, 86–9, 91–5, 100–1, 103–5, 118–19
Rome 115–16, 121–4

Sappho 35–7, 118
scholarship 5–7, 15–16, 21–8, 37–44
Scodel, Ruth 122
Serapis 67–8
Simonides 49–51, 117
Smyrna 100
Sotades 105–6
Sparta 76, 92–4

symposion 1–2, 76
Syracuse 107–8, 121

Telchines 28–30
Theocritus 83, 121
Thera 2, 70, 92–4
Theseus 52–6, 86–7
Thomas, Richard 122
Tithonus 35–6
trees 58–64, 82–3

Virgil 121–4

wealth and poverty 52–3
wrestling 61
writing *see* books and writing

Xerxes 118

Zephyrion 47, 66, 99–101, 102, 116
Zeus 25, 32, 75–9, 81, 93, 103–6